Questioning the Author

An Approach for Enhancing Student Engagement with Text

Isabel L. Beck
University of Pittsburgh
Pittsburgh, Pennsylvania, USA

Margaret G. McKeown
University of Pittsburgh
Pittsburgh, Pennsylvania, USA

Rebecca L. Hamilton
Pittsburgh Public Schools
Pittsburgh, Pennsylvania, USA

Linda Kucan
Bethany College
Bethany, West Virginia, USA

INTERNATIONAL READING ASSOCIATION
800 Barksdale Road, PO Box 8139,
Newark, Delaware 19714–8139, USA

The International Reading Association attempts, through its publications, to provide a forum for a wide spectrum of opinions on reading. This policy permits divergent viewpoints without implying the endorsement of the Association.

Director of Publications   Joan M. Irwin
Assistant Director of Publications   Wendy Lapham Russ
Senior Editor   Christian A. Kempers
Associate Editor   Matthew W. Baker
Assistant Editor   Janet S. Parrack
Editorial Assistant   Cynthia C. Sawaya
Association Editor   David K. Roberts
Production Department Manager   Iona Sauscermen
Graphic Design Coordinator   Boni Nash
Design Consultant   Larry F. Husfelt
Electronic Publishing Supervisor   Wendy A. Mazur
Electronic Publishing Specialist   Anette Schütz-Ruff
Electronic Publishing Specialist   Cheryl J. Strum
Electronic Publishing Assistant   Peggy Mason

Library of Congress Cataloging in Publication Data
    Questioning the author: An approach for enhancing student engagement with text / Isabel L. Beck ... [et al.].
        p.   cm.
    Includes bibliographical references and index.
    1. Reading comprehension.   2. Questioning.   3. Discussion.
4. Constructivism (Education)   I. Beck, Isabel L.
    LC1573.7.Q84   1997   96-52260
    372.47—dc21
    ISBN 0-87207-242-8

Fifth Printing, January 1999

CONTENTS

FOREWORD

Dear Reader,

I am pleased to share with you a book that, in my opinion, offers the most promising help for improving reading comprehension to appear in my career as an educator and researcher. I have been following Beck et al.'s work on "Questioning the Author" (QtA) for several years and I am delighted to see the approach become widely accessible to teachers and researchers in the form of an IRA publication.

Questioning the Author will be an exciting discovery for teachers who

- want their students to be able to understand and learn from all kinds of text;
- believe that students should construct meaning rather than retrieve information from what they read;
- see understanding text as an exciting collaborative effort involving students and teacher; and
- want students to be engrossed in rich discussions about what they are reading.

The QtA approach empowers both students and teachers. With QtA, students assume a greater responsibility for their own learning. Students do not just learn to locate and extract information from text. Rather, they "interact with text," "grapple with ideas," "become involved in issues," "investigate," "analyze," "clarify," "challenge," "refine," and "connect." With QtA, teachers, too, assume a greater role. Instead of simply assigning and assessing, teachers are actively engaged with students in exciting collaborative discussions about the meaning of text. Teachers become "facilitators" and "navigators"; they "orchestrate instruction," "ignite thinking," and "monitor understanding."

Questioning the Author has my enthusiastic support for three reasons. First, the approach is firmly founded on theory and research. With the cognitive theory of constructivism at its core, this publication is the logical culmination of the senior authors' prolific and impressive two-decade program of research in reading and learning from text. The QtA approach represents applied research at its finest.

My second reason for touting *Questioning the Author* is that it is a very practical guide. Classroom-tested for over three years, the approach is ready for widespread implementation. Teachers wishing to try QtA will find many helpful examples of actual classroom lessons, as well as other practical tips for using QtA in the classroom.

A third reason for promoting *Questioning the Author* is that it is very well-written. Ironically, the QtA approach is based on the premise that authors are fallible and that readers must work to understand the message. Readers of this book, however, will NOT have to question these authors or struggle for comprehension. This book is clear, succinct, and reader-friendly for both teachers and researchers.

I hope that you will find *Questioning the Author* as inspiring and hopeful as I have. It offers concrete and realistic help to teachers facing the challenge of helping students understand and learn from the texts they read. Best wishes for implementing QtA in your classrooms!

Sincerely yours,

Bonnie B. Armbruster
University of Illinois at Urbana–Champaign

ACKNOWLEDGMENT

The development of the material in this book was supported by funds from the Office of Educational Research and Improvement (OERI), the United States Department of Education, with additional funds from the Spencer Foundation. The opinions expressed do not necessarily reflect the position or policy of OERI or the Spencer Foundation, and no official endorsement should be inferred.

With much gratitude, we acknowledge the contributions of our researcher and teacher colleagues for all the effort and insight they brought to the design, development, and everyday working of Questioning the Author: Chris Cortinovos, Lisa Donovan, Linda Perhacs, Wendy Salvatore, Cheryl Sandora, Kelly Sweeney, Donald Weisz, and Jo Worthy.

INTRODUCTION

How many teachers have heard or expressed the following sentiment: "I've spent all week teaching this chapter and the students just aren't getting it"? That students do not "get it" is a common concern among educators. Despite the best efforts of teachers and the seeming attentiveness of students, students often fail to understand the ideas presented in their textbooks. In particular, students often are unable to connect the ideas they have encountered to information that is presented later. As one teacher expressed with frustration, "Sometimes the kids learn something; they even seem to know it for the test, and then, a month later, it's like they've never even heard of it!"

Because the concern about reading comprehension is so widespread, the following example of a brief passage from a textbook (Silver Burdett & Ginn, 1985, p. 106) and a student's response to it probably will not be much of a surprise. We offer the example simply to underscore what students may understand or fail to understand from reading their texts. The passage follows:

> **The French and Indian War.** In 1763 Britain and the colonies ended a 7-year war with the French and Indians. As a result of this war France was driven out of North America. Britain would now rule Canada and other lands that had belonged to France. This brought peace to the American colonies. The colonists no longer had to fear attacks from Canada. The Americans were happy to be a part of Britain in 1763. Yet a dozen years later, these same people would be fighting the British for independence, or freedom from Great Britain's rule. This war was called the War for Independence, or the American Revolution. A revolution changes one type of government or way of thinking and replaces it with another.

Think for a moment how the events described in the passage might be summarized. A summary might include the fact that the British fought a war against the French and their Indian allies; that Britain won the war, which meant that the French gave up their colonies in North America; and that the American colonists were happy about this outcome, although they also would be at war with Britain shortly. Now, consider how a fourth grader summarized the passage:

> There was a war in 1763 that Britain attacked to Canada. The government explained that there won't be no more attacks. And for a dozen years there hasn't been attacks in Canada for a dozen years.

The student seems to have understood very little from her reading. She learned a few words but was unable to use them in the correct context. For example, she says that Britain attacked Canada and that the government spoke out against attacks. This type of response to text raises the questions "Why does this happen?" and "What can we do about it?" The short answer to the question of why students often do not understand what they read is that students often do not interact with the text in ways that help them build understanding; that is, they do not actively engage with the information in the text. The short answer to what can we do about it is why we developed Questioning the Author (QtA), an approach designed to establish student interactions with text in a way that encourages them to engage with text ideas so they can build understanding.

The purpose of this book is to expand on our short answers to the two very important questions presented in the previous paragraph. We do this by exploring why students often take away little meaningful information from their reading and by describing how and why QtA addresses this problem.

We have divided the book into six chapters. In Chapter 1 we address what QtA is by discussing its purpose and describing its characteristics. Further, we differentiate QtA from other approaches that have some similar characteristics. We analyze examples of QtA in action in excerpts from lesson transcripts in an attempt to reveal reasons why some students are not successful in understanding text. We also describe the experiences that contributed to the development of QtA, the research that motivated its invention, and the theoretical orientation known as constructivism, the foundation upon which the QtA approach is built.

The next three chapters address specific QtA strategies for the classroom. Chapter 2 describes important QtA tools known as Queries and differentiates them from traditional questions. Then, Chapter 3 discusses the nature of planning for a QtA lesson, and Chapter 4 identifies important features of classroom discussion. In these three chapters, we also analyze lesson transcripts to develop an understanding of how to handle specific aspects of texts and to gain familiarity with techniques for QtA classroom discussions.

Chapter 5 discusses the implementation of QtA and presents procedures and tools to introduce students to the kinds of interactions QtA requires.

Finally, we conclude with Chapter 6, which presents an overview of QtA implementation with teachers and students in two school districts and a prospectus for the next phase of our collaboration with teachers.

It is our hope that the account of our work described in this book will provide not only some insights into the complexity of changing teaching practices to a more constructivist orientation but also will offer some insights into the possibilities for supporting such change in today's classrooms. Specifically, we hope that sharing what we have learned from teachers and students over the past five years will support teachers in their efforts to engage students in meaningful interactions with text.

CHAPTER 1

WHAT IS QUESTIONING THE AUTHOR AND HOW WAS IT DEVELOPED?

WHAT IS QUESTIONING THE AUTHOR?

Questioning the Author (QtA) is an approach for text-based instruction that is designed to facilitate building understanding of text ideas. The diagram in Figure 1 captures the key aspects of QtA. As the diagram shows, QtA assists students in building understanding through the use of Queries and discussion.

FIGURE 1   QUESTIONING THE AUTHOR: AN OVERVIEW

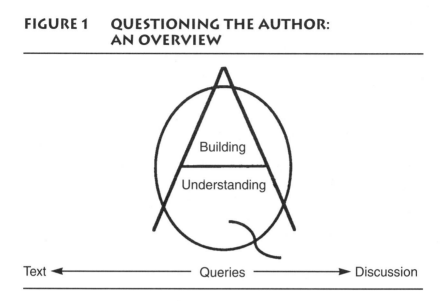

Text ◄——————————— Queries ——————————► Discussion

Building understanding is currently viewed as what a reader needs to do to read successfully. It is important to consider that building understanding is not extracting information from the page, which is how reading was once characterized. Rather, building understanding involves determining what information means. Reading is constructing meaning. The difference between thinking of reading as extracting information and an emphasis on constructing meaning is important in understanding QtA, and will be discussed in greater detail when we consider the topic of constructivism.

Notice the label *Text* on the diagram in Figure 1. QtA is an approach that is used for teaching about ideas in text. When students read a text in a QtA lesson, they are taught to address text ideas immediately while they are reading. As students are reading a text, they are taught to consider meaning, to develop and grapple with ideas, and to try to construct meaning. This is quite different from asking students to answer questions about a text after they have finished reading it.

The way QtA supports immediate construction of meaning is through *Discussion*. Classroom discussion is certainly not a new idea. However, the purpose for discussion in QtA and the kinds of interactions in which students engage during discussion depart from what is traditionally seen in classrooms. Classroom discussions are typically characterized by students' sharing of their opinions and ideas, but this is not exactly what happens in a QtA discussion. Students are not encouraged to share ideas they already have but rather to collaboratively construct ideas from what they are reading. The important and somewhat subtle difference between the two activities will be discussed in more depth later. For now, consider that, in more traditional discussions, students usually have already read a text and formulated their own thoughts and opinions about the text's meaning. In a QtA discussion, the goal is to assist students in the process of constructing meaning from a text; therefore, the discussion takes place in the course of reading the text for the first time so students can share in the experience of meaning construction as it is happening.

Finally, as indicated in Figure 1, the word *Queries* appears between the words *Text* and *Discussion*. *Queries* is placed there strategically because in a QtA lesson the interaction of text and discussion is accomplished through Queries. Queries are general probes the teacher uses to initiate discussion. The goal of Queries is to prompt students to consider meaning and develop ideas rather than to retrieve information and state ideas. Queries tend to be open ended and author oriented, and they place the responsibility for thinking and building meaning on students. Some examples of Queries are "So, what is the author trying to tell us?" or "Why is the author telling us that?" We will talk more about Queries in the next chapter, but for now it is important to know that they are a key instructional tool in QtA discussions that assist students in building understanding, or constructing meaning, from text.

QtA is an approach that can be used with either expository or narrative texts. *Expository* texts are informational
texts, including classroom textbooks that are used for teaching content areas such as social studies and science. *Narrative* texts are fictional selections such as stories, novels,
and fables, that typically involve characters attempting to
resolve a conflict. Many elementary school teachers who are
responsible for teaching reading often use an anthology of
both narrative and expository selections; for teaching sub-
jects such as social studies or science, they often use a
textbook with mostly expository text. QtA is a useful approach for both types of text.

The following is a brief synopsis of how QtA works: As text
is read in class, the teacher intervenes at selected points
and poses Queries to prompt students to consider information in the text. Students respond by contributing ideas, which
may be built upon, refined, or challenged by other students
and by the teacher. Finally, students and the teacher work collaboratively, interacting to grapple with ideas and build understanding. We will elaborate on this process of collaborative
meaning making while reading text throughout this book.

HOW DID QUESTIONING THE AUTHOR DEVELOP?

The principle of building understanding is fundamental to
QtA. This orientation comes from the past 25 years of research on learning, which has been termed the "cognitive
revolution" (Gardner, 1985). The research from this cognitive
perspective—investigations into how the mind works—
shows that in order to understand something, learners need
to actively use information, rather than simply collect pieces
of information. This view of learning is called *constructivism*
and emphasizes that learners need to act on information to
construct meaning in order for learning to take place (see, for
example, Beck & Carpenter, 1986; Bruer, 1993; Cohen,

McLaughlin, & Talbert, 1993; McGilly, 1994; Newman, Griffin, & Cole, 1989; Prawat, 1992; Resnick & Klopfer, 1989).

Constructing meaning is not a new way to describe an older notion of comprehension, which is to simply extract information. Rather, constructivism is a profoundly different view of processing information. According to a constructivist view, learning cannot happen simply by getting information from a source; understanding cannot be extracted from a text and put into a student's head, nor can it be delivered to a learner.

The cognitive perspective emphasizes the importance of a reader's efforts to interact with the information in a text in order to make sense of it (see, for example, Anderson, 1977; Beck, 1989; Beck & Carpenter, 1986; Kieras, 1985; Palincsar & Brown, 1989; Rumelhart, 1980; Schank & Abelson, 1977; van Dijk & Kintsch, 1983). Reading is understood to be a complex process in which a reader must draw on information from several sources concurrently to construct meaning from a text. As a reader progresses through a text, he or she attends to the information and combines it with knowledge of word meanings and language conventions, knowledge about the form of texts, and general knowledge relating to the content. The reader must identify each new piece of text information and decide how it relates to information already given. As reading proceeds, a reader forms a representation of the text's message and continually updates it as subsequent text information is encountered. The representation is formed by drawing connections between outside knowledge and text information and between given and new text information (see, for example, Clark, 1977; Clark & Haviland, 1977).

The difference between a constructivist view of reading and a former view of reading as a more passive collection of information from a text can be drawn sharply by considering what is taken as evidence of a reader's understanding within each view. From the older view, responding to ques-

---

tions with answers that could be retrieved directly from a text would be evidence of understanding; from a constructivist view, understanding involves being able to explain the information, connect it to previous knowledge, and use the information subsequently.

CONSTRUCTIVISM IN ACTION

The following example illustrates a constructivist view of understanding. Wendy became interested in schooners after watching the movie *Mutiny on the Bounty*. She bought posters, started to read Herman Melville, and decorated her bedroom with nautical paraphernalia. For her 13th birthday, Wendy's mother bought her a model of a 19th-century schooner, the type of model that comes in a huge box with hundreds of pieces. Wendy was thrilled and announced confidently to her mother that, considering all she had learned about ships, she would have the model assembled in a few days. Six months later, Wendy was still working on it.

Even after studying and reading about schooners, Wendy admitted to her mother that she had acquired only a superficial understanding of them and that, without constructing the model, she might never have known how superficial it was. She showed her mother how surprisingly the pieces would sometimes connect together, told her about the unexpected discoveries of the important functional nature of parts that at first seemed unimportant, and came to realize the necessity of collaborating with her sister and referring to the instruction manual for the model. Constructing the model demanded thinking and attention that Wendy had never needed or been challenged to use before.

We want students to construct a model of text and have opportunities to interact with texts the way Wendy did with the model ship. We want students to figure out what information is important and how the ideas connect. This kind of construction involves more than just receiving or reciting what is read or heard. Using the model ship analogy, the difference between getting meaning and constructing meaning is captured in the difference between Wendy's receiving the ship already constructed as opposed to constructing it herself. Wendy would have appreciated receiving a completed ship, but she would never have been able to understand as much about it as she did by building it herself.

CONSTRUCTIVISM IN READING

To demonstrate the notion of constructing meaning as it applies to reading, we look at a transcript that offers some examples of student responses to questions about what they are reading. In the first example, from a class in which students had been studying the climate and geography of Antarctica, the following excerpt from a social studies textbook (Laidlaw, 1985, p. 87) is read:

> Antarctica is one of the coldest places on earth. The temperature never gets above 32 degrees. This is because of the great ice buildup there, and because when Antarctica gets sun, the rays are more slanted than in most places.... In winter, the sun never shines. But in the summer, the sun shines 24 hours a day.

After the text is read, the teacher asks the following question: "When the sun shines 24 hours a day, why don't things warm up?" Two students repond:

Student 1: Because it's too cold. It never gets more than 32 degrees.

Student 2: Because even though the sun is shining, it's only slanted rays of the sun. So it looks like the sun is shining, but the rays can't warm it up like if it were right under the sunlight.

Consider the differences in the responses of the two students. The first student responds by simply extracting the text information that the temperature is below freezing. Although what she says is correct, it completely omits the explanation for the coldness, which is that Antarctica gets only slanted rays from the sun.

In contrast, the second student identifies and explains the slanted rays as the cause of the cold summer temperatures despite the 24 hours of sunlight. This student demonstrates an understanding of how the slanted rays relate to the seemingly contradictory situation of constant sunshine and cold temperatures. He constructs meaning by reaching beyond retrieval and repetition of text information to using text information to build an understanding of an important idea.

In another example, the following excerpt from the book *Mama's Bank Account* by Kathryn Forbes, which describes an immigrant's arrival in America, is read:

> It had been a long trip from Norway to San Francisco. But from the moment she stepped off the ferryboat, confused and lonely in a strange land, San Francisco was to become suddenly and uniquely her own.
>
> "Is like Norvay," she had declared. And straightaway she'd taken the city to her heart.

The teacher opens discussion by asking, "So what has the author told us about Mama?" Two students respond:

Student 1: She came from Norway to San Francisco, and when she got off the boat in San Francisco, she thought it looked just like Norway.

Student 2: From the first time she saw San Francisco, even though it was a brand new place for her, it felt like home. She said that it looked like Norway, her home that she came from.

Although the first student simply picks up some of the facts from the text, the second student combines some of the ideas to understand that the author is describing Mama's immediate attachment to San Francisco. Both students note the similarity that Mama saw between her old home (Norway) and her new home (San Francisco). However, the first student merely repeats text information about this similarity, whereas the second student interprets the text information to build the understanding that not only did San Francisco look like Norway, but it also felt like it.

These examples illustrate some of the differences between extracting information and constructing meaning from texts. In both examples, the students who gave the second response considered the information in the text and used it to make sense of the ideas rather than just locating information in the text and retrieving it in response to questions. Because of their constructive activity, both of the students who responded second in the examples were able to reveal the understanding of the text that they had built.

BACKGROUND RESEARCH ON TEXT AND READERS

Constructivism provided the basic foundation for developing QtA. However, it was current research in reading and our own work with social studies textbooks and young students' responses to them that provided the detailed information we needed to figure out what QtA would have to do to guide and support student meaning making from text.

Our own research on texts used understandings from cognitive research on reading as a basis from which to investigate how well students understood their textbooks. In particular, research findings about factors that can interfere with the reading process (see, for example, Just & Carpenter, 1987; Perfetti, 1985) guided our investigation. These factors include particular features of text that inhibit a reader's ability to make connections among ideas and a reader's failure to use prior knowledge to make sense of text ideas. For example, a reader's comprehension may be limited if the reader lacks knowledge of certain word meanings or knowledge relating to the topic of the text or fails to recognize that particular knowledge is relevant to the text (see, for example, Anderson et al., 1977; Beck, McKeown, & Omanson, 1987; Beck, Omanson, & McKeown, 1982; Omanson et al., 1984; Pearson, Hansen, & Gordon, 1979). A text may also cause problems for a reader if it includes ambiguous or indirect references, lacks information that sets up an appropriate context for the content, lacks clear connections between events or ideas, includes irrelevant events and ideas, or presents a high density of concepts (see, for example, Black & Bern, 1981; Bransford & Johnson, 1973; Haviland & Clark, 1974; Kintsch & Keenan, 1973; Trabasso, Secco, & van den Broek, 1984).

Our research on social studies texts began with an analysis of current textbooks. Our approach was to consider the kind of learning that students would be able to develop given the material in the text and students' level of background knowledge. We concluded that the textbooks we examined were ineffective in several important ways: they had unclear content goals, assumed more extensive prior background knowledge than readers actually had, and provided inadequate explanations (Beck, McKeown, & Gromoll, 1989). When we asked students to read some of the textbook passages, we found that they had difficulty constructing meaning from the content (Beck, McKeown, & Sinatra, 1989). Students typically recalled some facts or scattered details, but they were much less likely to understand the central ideas of what they had read.

In subsequent work, we developed revised versions of textbook passages that presented content more coherently by explaining connections among events, their causes, and their consequences. Our findings indicated that students had greater understanding of the ideas presented in the revised versions (Beck, McKeown, Sinatra, & Loxterman, 1991). The students were better able to recall the causes of important events and connections between events and to answer more open-ended questions correctly.

To develop the revised versions of text passages, we read the original passages, trying to understand the author's goal for the passage and what each idea was supposed to contribute to the goal. Then we formed our understandings into more coherent, clearer text statements. As we worked through texts in this way, we realized that our efforts to make connections and grapple with ideas were exactly the kinds of efforts we would want young readers to make in order to construct meaning from their texts. It occurred to us that we could encourage a constructivist orientation to reading by giving students a "reviser's eye." It is a reviser's task to make text understandable, and we intended for students to make text understandable to themselves. If students understood that their task as readers was to make what they read understandable, it might promote the kind of active engagement in reading that is needed for learning to take place.

TAKING ACTIVE ENGAGEMENT INTO INSTRUCTION

The goal of getting students actively involved in reading has received much attention from reading researchers and educators. This attention has been reflected in the development of several instructional approaches. One approach has been to encourage students to respond to what they read through collaborative discussion. A number of different approaches to fostering collaborative discussion have been developed, such as the Reflective Thinking Project (Anderson et al., 1992), the Book Club Project (McMahon et al., 1992), the Conversational Discussion Groups Project (O'Flahavan & Stein, 1992), Instructional Conversations (Goldenberg, 1992), and the Junior Great Books reading and discussion program (Denis & Moldof, 1983). A major difference between discussion in these approaches and in QtA is that the discussions take place after reading in these approaches. Thus, the ongoing process of constructing meaning that occurs *during* reading is not addressed.

Other work that encourages readers to assume more active roles has focused on the teaching, modeling, and practicing of strategies used by mature readers as they read. Several different teaching strategies and methods have been proposed, such as reciprocal teaching (Palincsar & Brown, 1984), informed strategies for learning (Paris, Cross, & Lipson, 1984), direct explanation (Duffy et al., 1987), transactional instruction (Pressley et al., 1992), and cognitive process instruction (Gaskins et al., 1993). A potential drawback of strategy-based instruction, however, is that the attention of teachers and students may be drawn too easily to the features of the strategies themselves rather than to the meaning of what is being read. In fact, some researchers have questioned the necessity of emphasizing specific strategies if the goal of reading as an active search for meaning could be kept in mind (see, for example, Carver, 1987; Dole et al., 1991; Pearson & Fielding, 1991).

Another way to activate readers' engagement is to promote an active search for meaning. This involves directing students to explain to themselves the information presented in their textbooks as they read. Chi and her colleagues have found that self-explanations can be elicited from students and that when they are, students are better able to learn the material presented to them (Chi et al., 1989; Chi et al., 1994).

QtA shares features with these other approaches to learning from text. However, its uniqueness lies in combining collaboration with immediate, explanatory responses during reading and adding a perspective that emphasizes the fallibility of an author, a notion that will be discussed in the following section.

A CLOSER LOOK AT QUESTIONING THE AUTHOR

Given the importance and the effectiveness of constructing meaning during reading, how do you get students to become actively involved as they read, to dive into difficult information and grapple to make sense of it? This question leads to a more detailed diagram of QtA that offers a more in-depth look at the process. In Figure 1, we described QtA as an approach that is designed to assist students in building understanding of the ideas in a text through the use of Queries and discussion. The new features added to the diagram in Figure 2 begin to explain how QtA prompts students to react to their texts in a different way.

**FIGURE 2   QUESTIONING THE AUTHOR:
A CLOSER LOOK**

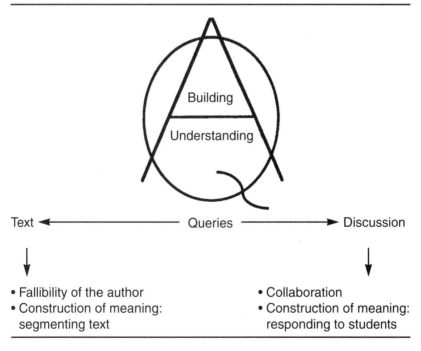

Text ⟵————————— Queries ————————⟶ Discussion

• Fallibility of the author
• Construction of meaning: segmenting text

• Collaboration
• Construction of meaning: responding to students

Notice the phrase *Fallibility of the author* under *Text*. *Fallibility of the author* represents an important issue that influences the way students attend to and deal with information in a text (Luke, DeCastell, & Luke, 1983; Olson, 1980). Textbooks carry authority in the classroom by virtue of their central role in the curriculum. Thus, textbooks are often viewed by students and teachers as above criticism. So when students have difficulty understanding the content of their textbooks, they tend to attribute these difficulties to their own inadequacies as readers. One way that students can avoid blaming themselves is to disengage from the reading process—to merely skim over what they read and apply less effort because not to try is not to fail.

An important mechanism for helping students engage with text in QtA is to depose the authority of the text. Our starting point in QtA is to let students know that the book's content is simply someone's ideas written down, and that this person may not have always expressed things in the clearest or easiest way for readers to understand. Armed with the view of an author as a human being who is potentially fallible, students can view texts as less impersonal, authoritative, and incomprehensible.

Over time, we have found that students begin to understand that it may be an author's fallibility in communicating ideas that is the problem rather than their lack of ability to comprehend the ideas. This understanding tends to change both the reaction and the responsibility of the student because it shifts the blame for not comprehending from the student to the author. As a result of shifting that blame, students tend to feel more confident in working to understand text and more willing to grapple with ideas as they read. QtA is aimed at teaching students that they can become skilled at figuring out what an author might have meant to say at various points in the text by thinking and wrestling with meaning.

Another major concept in QtA, as shown in Figure 2, is *construction of meaning* during reading. In QtA, we teach students that readers must try to "take on" a text little by little, idea by idea, and try to understand while they are reading what ideas are there and how they might connect or relate those ideas. To understand this approach, consider what is often done in classrooms when teaching from a text. It is typical practice to assign material to be read and then to pose questions to evaluate student comprehension. This read-question-evaluate pattern is an "after-the-fact" procedure. There are two problems with this approach. First, students may have questions as they read or may simply finish a text knowing only that they are lost but are not sure why. The questions posed by the teacher only serve to expose their embarrassment over their lack of understanding. Also, there is no way for teachers to know if some students have constructed misconceptions about the passage and think they have understood. Second, even though students hear right answers, they may never understand what makes them right.

In QtA, however, the goal is to assist students in their efforts to understand as they are reading for the first time. Not only is this orientation a better reflection of how a reader needs to address text content to build understanding, but it is also an opportunity for valuable teaching and learning experiences. First, it gives teachers repeated opportunities to facilitate student efforts as they are trying to understand what they are reading. Teachers can model confusion, identify problematic language and difficult ideas in text, and ask Queries that focus student thinking. All these actions can serve as comprehension strategies that students ultimately learn and use on their own. Second, grappling during reading gives students the opportunity to hear from one another, to question and consider alternative possibilities, and to test their own ideas in a safe environment. Everyone is grappling, everyone is engaged in constructing meaning, and everyone understands that the author, not the teacher, has presented them with this challenge. The chance for cumulative misconceptions diminishes, and the opportunity for meaningful discussion increases.

Constructing meaning during reading means going back and forth between reading relatively small segments of text and discussing the ideas encountered. This back and forth process requires decisions about where to stop reading a text and to begin discussion of ideas. It is the task of a teacher using the QtA approach to prepare for this construction of meaning by analyzing and identifying the important concepts of a text and making decisions about how much of the text needs to be read at once and why. Making decisions about how much text to read is referred to as *segmenting* text, that is, identifying starting and stopping points. Decisions about segmenting the text are made based on the text content and the ideas and information presented, not on the length of a page or the point at which a page or a paragraph ends. Later, when we address planning, we will discuss in greater detail how to make decisions about where to segment a text and how to introduce the concept of author fallibility to students.

Discussion, as indicated in Figure 2, is another key aspect of QtA. Remember that the goal of QtA is to get students to grapple with an author's ideas and, if necessary, to challenge an author's intended meaning in an effort to build understanding. To accomplish this, students must be involved in thinking and talking. Therefore, we need to hear student voices, encourage their contributions, and urge them to wrestle with ideas. Students need to learn the power of collaborating with their peers and teachers to construct meaning.

Consider an example of discussion and collaboration. Think of the last good movie you saw. When you came out of the theater with your friends, you were probably discussing the film, arguing with one another about what it really meant, offering reasons about why you liked it or hated it, why it made you laugh or cry, or what the true significance

---

and message of the film was. Such interaction is natural and extremely valuable in constructing meaning. Students need to engage in these same kinds of interactions when they read, considering and reacting to their peers' ideas and supporting their own arguments.

Although discussion is a key aspect of QtA, we do not view discussion itself as the goal. Rather, discussion in a QtA lesson is the means toward achieving a goal, and that goal is always the same: constructing meaning. As students learn to challenge an author, they learn to challenge and be challenged by one another as well. It is the attempt to understand the text, not the activity of arguing ideas or topics, that is most important.

Perhaps one of the ways to best understand this distinction is to remember that unlike in most classroom discussions, the teacher using QtA is actively involved. This is different from, for example, a Junior Great Books discussion in which a teacher sets a discussion in motion and the students explore an issue. In QtA, the teacher is in the discussion the entire time, as a facilitator, guide, initiator, and responder. This is why the words *responding to students* are found on the diagram in Figure 2 . QtA provides an important and extremely interactive role for the teacher. The whole class, including the teacher, is constructing meaning during a QtA lesson. The teacher is attentive and responsive to the students' comments in order to guide the discussion in productive ways.

The next chapter focuses on Queries, the prompts that inititate student interactions with text ideas and support student efforts to construct meaning from those ideas.

CHAPTER 2

QUERIES

Queries are a key aspect of Questioning the Author (QtA), as mentioned in the previous chapter. They link text and discussion and are a driving force in helping students build understanding, or construct meaning, from text. Because of the important role they play, Queries are the focus of this chapter.

HOW QUERIES DIFFER FROM SOME TRADITIONAL QUESTIONS

We begin by considering what Queries are and what appears to differentiate them from some traditional questions. The major points of comparison are summarized in Table 1. One difference between questions and Queries is that some questions are used to assess student comprehension of text information after reading. In contrast, Queries are designed to assist students in grappling with text ideas as they construct meaning.

In Chapter 1 we referred to a typical pattern of instruction in which students read a passage, the teacher initiates a series of questions, students respond, and the teacher evaluates their responses. This pattern, which has been documented as a prevalent teaching practice, is referred to as the IRE pattern of instruction: Initiate, Respond, and Evaluate (Dillon, 1988; Mehan, 1979). The IRE pattern *assesses* comprehension; it does not *assist* the process of comprehending. Moreover, the IRE pattern of asking questions after the reading is completed tends to involve questions that are more effective in encouraging students to recall what they have read rather than in supporting students as they build an understanding of what they are reading.

Queries, in contrast, are less focused on assessing and evaluating student responses than on supporting students as they dig in to make sense of what they are reading. Queries focus attention on the quality and depth of the meaning that students are constructing rather than on the accuracy of the responses they give.

TABLE 1 CHARACTERISTICS OF SOME TRADITIONAL QUESTIONS AND QtA QUERIES

Questions	Queries
1. assess student comprehension of text information after reading	1. assist students in grappling with text ideas to construct meaning
2. evaluate individual student responses to teacher's questions and prompt teacher-to-student interactions	2. facilitate group discussion about an author's ideas and prompt student-to-student interactions
3. are used before or after reading	3. are used during initial reading

As indicated in Table 1, another difference between questions and Queries is that the purpose of some traditional questions seems to be to evaluate individual student responses and to prompt teacher-to-student interactions. In contrast, Queries aim to facilitate group discussion about an author's ideas and tend to prompt student-to-student interactions.

Questions are often useful in giving teachers a quick idea of which students are comprehending text and which are not. However, what also tends to happen is that, although a question is directed to the entire class, only one student provides the answer. This individual assumes all the responsibility and releases the other students from any share in it. The action takes place between the teacher and one student, and the rest of the class is not involved. Students tend to compete for the chance to say the right answer, and the teacher lets students know when their answers are correct.

Queries, on the other hand, are designed to change the role of the teacher to a facilitator of discussion. A teacher who uses Queries evaluates student responses less often and focuses more on encouraging students to consider an author's ideas and to respond to one another's interpretations of those ideas. As a result, student-to-student and student-to-teacher interactions tend to increase, and the context for learning is a classroom of spirited learners grappling with an author's text and working together to understand it.

Our last point, as noted in the table, is that questions typically are used before or after reading. In contrast, Queries are used continually during the initial reading of a text. When teachers ask questions after reading, students may get messages that teachers may not intend. For example, students may assume that questioning is a different and perhaps unrelated exercise from reading. Right and wrong is the focus of attention for both teacher as evaluator and student as evaluatee. Are these the messages we want to convey to students? A more correct message is that readers are always questioning as they read. Questioning and reading are symbiotically related, enhancing each other in mutually beneficial ways.

When teachers use Queries, students are more likely to get the message that reading and trying to determine the author's intended meaning are aspects of the same process. The thinking elicited by Queries is part of the reading experience, not something that is separate from that experience. Queries supplement the text, helping students deal with what is there as well as with what is not there. The focus of Queries is on building understanding, not on checking understanding.

COMPARING THE EFFECTS OF QUESTIONS AND QUERIES

To provide a better sense of the nature of Queries, what they are, what they accomplish, and how they differ from some traditional questions, we will consider an example of a question-driven lesson and an example of a Query-driven lesson. The first example is based on an excerpt from a social studies textbook about early Polynesians that was used in a fourth-grade class. We will look at a transcript of the lesson as it unfolded with the teacher's traditional questions driving the discussion. In the second example, we will show how the same text excerpt was handled 1 year later by the same teacher after she had learned about QtA and how Queries can be used to direct discussion. Finally, we will consider the difference in what students seem to understand as a result of a Query-driven lesson in contrast to a question-driven lesson.

Here is the excerpt about early Polynesians from a social studies textbook (Laidlaw, 1985, p. 148):

> When the Polynesians settled on the Hawaiian Islands, they began to raise plants that they had brought with them. One kind of plant that the Polynesians raised was the taro plant. This is a kind of plant raised in warm, wet lands, mostly for its roots. The early Hawaiians cooked the roots, and then they generally

---

pounded them on a board to make a paste called poi. This was a favorite food of the early Hawaiians. Sweet potatoes, bananas, breadfruit, and coconuts were some of the other plants that the early Hawaiians raised for food. Animals raised by the early Hawaiians for food were chickens, pigs, and dogs.

In the first example, to start the lesson, the teacher asks the question, "What did the early Hawaiians eat?" As indicated below, the students answer by naming things they read in the text, and the teacher repeats what each student says, sometimes interjecting other questions:

Rania: Sweet potatoes.

Teacher: Sweet potatoes. Excellent. Brent?

Brent: Breadfruit.

Teacher: Breadfruit. What is breadfruit? What is it? Is it bread? No, what is it? Carmen?

Carmen: A tree that has fruit.

Teacher: Yes. It's a tree that has a fruit. And when you cook the fruit, it looks like...

Jim: Bread.

Teacher: Bread. That's why we call it breadfruit, isn't it? And it has no seeds. Excellent. Good readers. Nakisha?

Nakisha: Coconut.

Teacher: Coconuts. Beth?

Beth: Bananas.

Teacher: Bananas. John?

John: Chicken.

Teacher: Chicken.

Nicole: Pigs.

Teacher: OK.

As the lesson proceeds, the students offer more examples of foods eaten by the early Polynesians, such as seaweed and roots. Then, the teacher asks questions that lead students to describe poi, the Hawaiians' favorite food, again through single-word responses, breaking the pattern only to elicit more information:

Jim: Seaweed.

Teacher: Seaweed. Kelvin?

Kelvin: Roots.

Teacher: Roots? What do you call those roots?

Kelvin: Uh. Poi.

Teacher: OK. What did we call the roots?

Jim: Taro.

Teacher: Good. Now, what did they make out of taro?

Jim: Poi.

Teacher: Poi. What's the Hawaiians' favorite food?

Jim: Poi.

Teacher: And what does it look like? How can we describe it? What's the poi look like, Nakisha?

Nakisha: Like paste.

Teacher: Paste. It doesn't taste like paste, goodness no, but it looks like paste. It has the same consistency, and it is called poi, and that was their favorite food. Did we miss anything, Nicole?

Nicole: Seafood.

Teacher: Seafood. I think we have it all. John?

John: They said they ate a kind of seaweed.

After naming all the foods, it is not clear if the students have any understanding of what this information means or how it connects to an important idea. Additionally, the tone of this lesson is dull and uneventful. There is a kind of monotonous pendulum-like effect, with the teacher and students echoing one another in one-word exchanges.

Now, we will look at how the same text excerpt was handled a year later by the same teacher, using Queries instead of questions to drive the lesson. Recall that the first time the teacher taught this lesson, she had the students read the entire text excerpt and then answer her questions. One year later, the lesson begins as follows, after the class had read just the first sentence of the text excerpt: "When the Polynesians settled on the Hawaiian Islands, they began to raise plants that they had brought with them." Then the teacher begins the discussion as follows:

Teacher: What does the author mean by just this one sentence?

Antonio: He means that they brought some of the food that they had there with them.

Antonio's response misses a key point that is essential to understanding the message of the paragraph: the Polynesians brought certain foods with them that they then began to raise in their new environment. The teacher's next Query emphasizes this point and leads to an important exchange with Temika:

Teacher: Um-hmm, we decided that yesterday. But what does the author mean by they began to *raise* the plants they brought with them. Temika?

Temika: Like the plants and stuff, they began to plant them.

Teacher: They began to plant them, why?

Temika: For their food!

Teacher: Right! They can plant the things that they brought, then they're going to have their own crops in Hawaii. OK, good.

When the important concept about raising crops is brought out, notice how the QtA orientation of digging into text information produces a question from a student:

Alvis: Why do they need to plant things when they already brought things over?

Alvis realizes that he does not understand the significance of the author's point. Notice that rather than answering the student herself, the teacher returns the responsibility for thinking and grappling with the issues to the students:

Teacher: Who can answer Alvis's question? He said, they already had food, why did they have to plant the food? Roberta?

Roberta: Maybe because, like back then in the Hawaiian Islands...probably, you couldn't drive to the store, like they do now.

Teacher: OK, so Roberta's saying they couldn't get in their car and drive to the stores, but Alvis still has a point: Why not just eat the food they brought?

Alvis: They could run out.

Teacher: Oh, I think you just answered your own question. Alvis, say what you just said.

Alvis: 'Cause they'll run out of food.

Turning back the question to students gives them a chance to rediscover the idea that food eventually runs out and that to survive the Hawaiians needed to plant their own crops. Roberta's explanation helps Alvis realize that the food may have run out. Once the issue has been resolved, the teacher is ready to continue. This segment of the lesson transcript suggests that the combination of deliberate segmenting of text based on the ideas in the text and a sequence of carefully developed Queries make it possible for students to grapple with important ideas.

The lesson proceeds with the reading of the remaining paragraphs. The teacher again begins discussion with an open-ended Query: "What's the author telling us in the rest of this paragraph?" This Query is aimed at getting students to notice the overall idea that the author is developing rather than the specific details (the list of foods) the author includes. It seems to work, as the remarks of two students provide a summary of the idea:

Antonio: Well, they're naming some of the things that they ate.

Roberta: The author's telling us plants or food, like the taro, the bananas. And they're telling us how they cooked it, and where they found it.

Teacher: Yes, they pounded it on a board to make a paste called poi.

Next, the teacher notices that an issue comes up in the text that addresses a concern the class had expressed in the previous day's discussion. Notice the teacher's reaction to the text sentence. She says, "Ah-hah! I think the author answered the question that someone had yesterday. What's the author telling us that we had a question about yesterday?" The next several exchanges indicate that students are deciding that the author has answered their question about eating dogs:

Aletha: We were concerned about the dogs, if they ate the dogs.

Teacher: What does the author tell us? Temika?

Temika: If they raise them then they eat them. It said the animals raised by the early Hawaiians for food...

(Students are talking at once.)

Teacher: Wait a minute, two or three paragraphs later the author gave us the answer. We had no idea why they brought the dogs over. And now we know, don't we? For food. And I thought maybe so, but now I know. OK, now let's not say it anymore. Let's just go on now.

The way the information is presented in the text prompts a question from another student:

> Roberta: My question is, the author told us, I think it was yesterday, that they raised chickens, pigs, and dogs. And he's telling us again. Why is he telling us again?

The teacher's response turns the responsibility for thinking about the question back to students. Roberta is then able to resolve her own issue in responding to the teacher's question:

> Teacher: That's a great question. Did the author tell us yesterday that the Polynesians *raised* chickens, pigs, and dogs? What did the author tell us yesterday?
>
> Roberta: They carried them.
>
> Teacher: They carried them. Some of us thought they brought them over to hunt with. Three paragraphs later, the author's telling us why they brought them.

These transcripts show three major points. First, traditional questions often tend to restrict and confine thinking. That is, by seeking specific answers, traditional questions ask students to retrieve information, not analyze or think about it. Second, instead of limiting students' thinking and the ideas in the text, Queries help clarify the author's ideas so students can grapple directly with them. The third point is that the kinds of questions teachers ask students can contribute to either engagement or disengagement with ideas; in other words, what teachers ask and expect of students influences students' understanding and engagement.

To capture some of the important differences between the two lessons about early Polynesians, a summary of some characteristics of the question-driven and the Query-driven discussions is presented in Table 2. First, the Query-driven discussion seemed to change student responses. In the question-driven discussion, students tended to respond in short, one-word answers, and they frequently used the author's language. In the Query-driven discussion, the students gave longer, more elaborate answers that reflected original thought and analysis expressed in the students' own language.

Second, the text orientation of the Query-driven discussion was different from the question-driven discussion. Students tended to use a text in the question-driven discussion as a resource for retrieving information, a place to check the facts against their own memories. The text was little more than a source for finding correct answers. In contrast, in the Query-driven discussion, the text seemed to take on a different role. It seemed to become a working reference for connecting ideas and analyzing an author's style and motivation. The text became an ally in constructing meaning.

TABLE 2   A COMPARISON OF QUESTION-DRIVEN AND QUERY-DRIVEN DISCUSSIONS ABOUT EARLY POLYNESIANS

Question-Driven Discussions	Query-Driven Discussions
Student Responses	
• one-word answers	• longer, more elaborate answers
• in author's language	• in student's language
Text Orientation	
• resource for retrieving information	• reference for connecting ideas
• source for finding correct answers	• ally in constructing meaning
Discussion Dynamics	
• teacher-to-student interactions	• student-to-student interactions
• dull pace: little student engagement	• exciting pace: student engagement
• product oriented	• process oriented
• all questions teacher initiated	• some questions student initiated

Third, there were differences in the dynamics of the question-driven and the Query-driven discussions. Questions tend to promote teacher-to-student interactions with few opportunities for students to respond to one another or debate issues. As a result, question-driven lessons had a dull pace with little student engagement. The question-driven discussion was product oriented, and the product was what students remembered or what they could find in the text.

In contrast, the Query-driven discussion tended to promote student-to-student interactions as well as student-to-teacher exchanges, a more natural context for considering ideas. The Query-driven discussion seemed to have an exciting pace, with evidence of student engagement. In addition, the Query-driven discussion was process oriented. The goal was not focused completely on getting the right answer; rather, the goal was to get involved in the process of approaching a text in ways that encourage deep thinking.

Finally, in the question-driven discussion, almost all questions were teacher initiated. In the Query-driven discussion, at least some questions were student initiated.

To summarize, we believe that there are distinct advantages to Query-driven discussions. In Query-driven discussions, students do the work; they construct the meaning, wrestle with the ideas, and consider the ways information connects to construct meaning. As in the lesson transcripts of the discussion about early Polynesians, Queries put the responsibility for figuring out the author's intended meaning on students. The discussion becomes an opportunity for students to formulate complete thoughts, respond to the text, react to one another's ideas, and collaboratively construct new understandings.

When a teacher uses Queries, text becomes an ally to students. Students refer to the text to verify, argue about, and interpret the ideas they have read about. A previously invisible author takes on a more visible role and becomes a partner in student attempts to understand text that is not easily understood. Students can begin to understand the text's role and their role in constructing meaning. The result is that students acquire a deeper understanding of major text ideas, and, just as importantly, they can begin to appreciate the power of reading and thinking and expressing ideas in a collaborative discussion.

TYPES OF QUERIES

We refer to Queries in QtA as either initiating or follow-up. We differentiate them in this way mostly because some Queries tend to be more effective in accomplishing certain goals, which will be explained in the following sections. These two kinds of Queries are not separate or fixed, with unrelated application and purpose; rather we use these labels only to provide a sense of how and when to use Queries.

INITIATING QUERIES

Three types of Initiating Queries are as follows:

- What is the author trying to say here?
- What is the author's message?
- What is the author talking about?

These Queries are suggested prompts to make text ideas public and to launch a discussion. Their purpose is more important than their wording. Initiating Queries are not step-by-step instructions for starting a discussion in QtA, nor do they offer a single direction for the discussion to follow. Rather, they provide guidance, perspective, and several possible ways for students to gain understanding through discussion. The major goals of Initiating Queries are to make public the messages or ideas presented by an author. They draw attention to the most important text ideas and remind students that those ideas were written by an author.

The following lesson transcript is from a social studies lesson about life in Siberia. The teacher begins by expressing concern about some sentences from the text and rereading those sentences:

Teacher: Hold on. I'm concerned about these sentences: "During the summer months these people spent time preparing reindeer meat. They also made cheese from reindeer milk. These foods were then stored for the long winter months." What's the author trying to tell us here? "These foods were then stored for the long winter months." Charles?

Students begin to respond, focusing mainly on it being too cold in Siberia to gather food in the winter. The teacher persists in trying to get the students to go beyond the words in the text and reach for greater meaning:

Charles: They, they had to gather up food because they um, because they'd need food for the winter since it's so cold.

Teacher: Oh, OK. Charles said 'cause it's so cold. I'm still a little confused. What do you think, Antonio?

Antonio: I think that the author thinks that during the summer months they had to go out and be gathering up the food 'cause it's not as cold but it's still cold. And then when it's winter, they don't have to worry about uh, trying to get their food.

Teacher: I think we're all agreeing that in the wintertime, they're not gonna get anything to eat, but I'm not sure I understand why. What do you think, Alvis?

Alvis: I think, I think they do it in the summer because in the winter it's too hard to find all the food, because there's a lot of snow. And the trees and the plants and everything are dead because it's too cold.

Tammy: I think that they store all their food because the animals like, go away for the winter. They can't find animals to kill because it's too cold.

Betty: I think that they do it in the summer because, I agree with Tammy, 'cause it's warmer so they can find animals.

The teacher then recaps the ideas students have suggested and points out that they—not the author—came up with the ideas:

Teacher: Those are really good ideas. The author just told us, "These foods were then stored for the long winter months." But did he tell us why?

Students: No.

Teacher: No. And Tammy thinks it's 'cause the reindeer kind of hibernate. Is that what you mean? And Alvis and Betty said it's because it's too cold for the hunters to hunt. And you know what? I don't really know the answer. But I think you have some good ideas that might possibly be why. And it's important that you were able to come up with those ideas.

In this example, the Initiating Query sets in motion a collaborative discussion in which students are doing something quite important—building an understanding of text ideas rather than retrieving text information. Gradually, as the contributions of Antonio, Alvis, Tammy, and Betty are combined with the teacher's summarizing, the students build the understanding that climate affects behavior and motivates action, and that the author did not express this idea very clearly. We do not believe that these understandings would have been as likely to be constructed without the Initiating Query that began the discussion.

To summarize, we observed three specific effects of the Initiating Query in the "life in Siberia" lesson. First, students did the work of constructing meaning. The teacher asked students to do the thinking and started a discussion and set things in motion with a clear goal in mind. She guided the students to a realization about the text, but she did not tell them what the realization was.

Second, students discovered the difference between knowing what an author says and knowing what an author means. They also helped one another get the job done; they needed to combine ideas, and with prompting and encouragement, they dug into the text more than once to unravel the meaning.

Finally, the tone of the interactions was positive; there was evidence of engagement and personal investment in ideas and thought. The students were learning, and they were enjoying the activity.

FOLLOW-UP QUERIES

The goals of Follow-up Queries are to help focus the content and direction of a discussion and to assist students in integrating and connecting ideas to construct meaning.

Two related Follow-up Queries that encourage students to consider the ideas behind an author's words—to look at what the text means rather than what the text says—are as follows:

- What does the author mean here?
- Does the author explain this clearly?

Follow-up Queries also help students connect ideas that have been learned or read previously. These Queries are particularly useful in guiding students to relate information from different parts of the text; they also help students see that a connection or linking piece of information may be missing from the text. Here are two examples:

- Does this make sense with what the author told us before?
- How does this connect to what the author told us here?

Finally, Follow-up Queries, such as those listed below, assist students in figuring out an author's possible reasons for including certain information:

- Does the author tell us why?
- Why do you think the author tells us this now?

The following example shows how meaning is built in a discussion using Follow-up Queries. The example is from a discussion about these two sentences in a social studies text (Laidlaw, 1985, p. 87): "There is no sunlight during most of the winter months in Antarctica. However, during the summer months the sun shines 24 hours a day." The teacher begins with an Initiating Query that draws a response that does not address the issue represented by the text:

Teacher: What's the author trying to tell us here?

Aletha: The earth keeps on going around, keep on going around 24 hours a day.

The teacher then poses a Follow-up Query that directly addresses the difficulty: the author is presenting information that conflicts with what the students already understand about night and day.

Teacher: Aletha says that the earth keeps going around, 24 hours a day. So right now on one side of the earth it's daylight, and over here it's dark (pointing on a globe). So what does the author mean when he says there's no sunlight during most of the winter, and the sun shines 24 hours a day in the summer?

Darleen: Um, I think it's like, um, every time it goes around from the light to dark, every time it goes around it changes from light to dark, every 24 hours.

Darleen's response misses the point, so the teacher presses with another Follow-up Query. The Query urges students to put the pieces of information together, which the next student called on begins to do very nicely:

Teacher: Well, I think Darleen's saying the same thing that a lot of you are saying, that the globe is turning around and when it's light on this side, it's dark over here. Does that make sense with what the author just told us?

Heidi: This part right here; it's summer now. And this part down here; it's winter, and it snows down here all the time 'cause there's no sun getting down there. Antarctica's right down here, and when the sun comes, Antarctica's getting sun and the sun's coming this way, and it's hitting Antarctica.

Building from Heidi's comment, the teacher recaps what the discussion has revealed so far and prompts students to consider if the author has explained why the sun works this way in Antarctica. The teacher then asks students to recall information that a student had mentioned in an earlier discussion:

Teacher: Heidi's added some important things. She said that when the globe's going around when it's winter down here, Antarctica never gets any sun, and when it's summer, Antarctica does get sun. Now it seems like that is what the author's telling us. But does the author tell us why?

Class: No.

Teacher: Think about this for a minute. There's something else that Amber said a little while back. She said there's something funny about the earth. It's not straight up and down.

The students begin to work out the explanation for Antarctica's pattern of sunshine and weather:

Tammy: It's tilted.

Teacher: It's tilted. Now how does that connect with what the author has told us here?

Brandy: It doesn't get as much sun in the winter, 'cause the sun has to come up under but it's tilted the other way in the summertime.

Thomas: I think he's saying, like Brandy said, it goes around for 24 hours a day and, here goes the sun, the sun shines on Antarctica, slanted, all the way around 24 hours a day.

Shanelle: Um, um, I think I know what they're saying because when, when the earth is going around and the sun is coming, it's hitting—the lower part of Antarctica is showing, 'cause it's tilting more. So then it has sunshine 24 hours.

As the teacher recaps student contributions, it seems clear that the students have indeed put all the information together, that is, that the tilt in the earth's axis explains the 24 hours of light in Antarctica.

Teacher: I think we've worked this out. What Shanelle and Thomas are saying is that because the earth is tilted when it's going around the sun, we got 24 hours of sunlight in the summer, 'cause the sun keeps hitting and keeps hitting Antarctica, even though this part of the globe is in darkness.

There are several specific effects of the Follow-up Queries in the "climate of Antarctica" transcript. First, we can see that with the teacher's guidance, the students were able to link past knowledge with new information in the text. Second, as the discussion unfolded, students built on one another's comments to unravel important information: the author was alluding to a scientific concept they had to understand before they could understand the text. Finally, meanings and explanations emerged from several sources, not only from the students, teacher, or text, but also from a collaboration that involved all three.

NARRATIVE QUERIES

In addition to Initiating and Follow-up Queries, we also have developed some Queries that take into account the special characteristics of narrative texts in terms of authorship, purpose, and structure to help students construct meaning. We developed these Queries because of the differences between narrative and expository texts.

Difference in authorship is one consideration in comparing these two types of texts. Authors of expository textbooks frequently are teams of content experts who are well versed in their specific fields but who may not be professional writers. These authors may not be as concerned with presentation, coherence, and eloquence of language as they are with accuracy and coverage of information. Conversely, authors of narrative texts generally are writers by craft. However, although they might be considered less fallible in the areas of presentation and eloquence, writers of narrative texts can nonetheless be difficult to understand. Some of the problems in understanding narrative texts are the same kinds of problems offered by expository texts, such as difficult language and unfamiliar and dense content.

Another feature to consider is the difference in purpose between expository text and narrative text. Expository text is intended to present information, and clarity and precision are the author's goals. Narrative texts, however, explore recurring literary themes in original and creative ways. Authors of narratives often use artful forms of expression that *suggest* rather than *demonstrate* meanings through the use of figurative language such as metaphor and idioms.

Finally, the structures of expository and narrative texts differ. The structure of expository texts, particularly textbooks, is often signaled by headings and subheadings. The structure of narrative texts may be less obvious, particularly when the elements of character, motivation, setting, foreshadowing, and flashbacks are taken into account.

There are four Queries that we have found to be particularly useful in addressing the unique aspects of narrative text. These first two Queries help students think about characters and their motivations:

- How do things look for this character now?
- Given what the author has already told us about this character, what do you think he's up to?

Two other Queries can be effective in focusing students' thinking on the author's crafting of the plot:

- How has the author let you know that something has changed?
- How has the author settled this for us?

In order to see how the additional Narrative Queries play out in an actual lesson, we will examine a series of brief exchanges taken from the transcript of a narrative text lesson. In this lesson, the class was reading an excerpt from the book *The Cricket in Times Square* by George Selden. In the part of the story that the students read in the prior lesson, Mario's pet cricket, Chester, had eaten half of a two dollar bill. This is quite a problem because to Mario's family, the Bellinis, two dollars is a lot of money. In the following paragraph from the story, Mario's mother, Mama Bellini, discovers what the cricket has done:

> Chester Cricket sat frozen to the spot. He was caught red handed, holding the chewed up two dollars in his front legs. Muttering with rage, Mama Bellini picked him up by his antennae, tossed him into the cricket cage, and locked the gate behind him. He half expected that she would pick him up, cage and all, and throw him onto the shuttle tracks.

The teacher begins with a Query that draws attention to Chester's situation. She asks, "How do things look for Chester?" Students paraphrase and explain the nature of Chester's trouble. Darleen, for example, answers, "[I]t looks like Chester's in a lot of trouble." Roberta adds that Chester is in trouble because "she was going to throw him out [on the] shuttle tracks." This paraphrasing suggests that the students have more than a superficial awareness of a situation; they have an understanding of it, which reflects a deeper grasp of its meaning.

As the story unfolds, Papa Bellini and his son Mario enter the scene. The class reads the following segment:

> A three-cornered conversation began. Mama denounced Chester as a money eater.... Papa said he didn't think Chester had eaten the two dollars on purpose... Mama said he had to go. Papa said he could stay, but he'd have to be kept in the cage. And Mario knew that Chester, like all people who were used to freedom, would rather die than live his life behind bars.

The teacher then poses the Query that prompts students to follow the plot twists: "How does the author let you know that something's changed a little bit?" Tammy verbalizes a pending conflict that will influence and drive the rest of the story in the following statement:

> Tammy: I think the author means that...the father... doesn't want Chester to leave...for Mama to hurt Chester or anything [and that the cage is like] being put in jail and Mario knew he wouldn't like that.

Tammy not only identifies the conflict, she also demonstrates her understanding of how the plot was constructed by the author.

Here is the segment of text that is discussed in another example of a lesson in which the teacher uses a Narrative Query:

> Finally it was decided that since the cricket was Mario's pet, the boy would have to replace the money. And when he had, Chester could come out again. Until then—the cage.

The teacher begins by reviewing some comments made earlier in the lesson: "So this is very interesting. Darleen said earlier that she saw an argument developing here, 'cause Papa said he had to stay in the cage, and Mario thought that'd be kind of miserable." Then she poses a Narrative Query highlighting that a conflict has been resolved: "So, how's the author settled that for us?"

Shanelle responds, "It has to do with the cage because the cricket Chester has to stay in the cage 'til Mario pays the two dollars." Shanelle identifies a milestone in the plot; by summarizing what the author has done to resolve an issue, she demonstrates an awareness of the plot's progression and an understanding about what is happening in the story and why.

In this next part of the story, Chester's animal friends get into the act:

> Harry Cat folded his front paws over each other and rested his head on them. "Let me get this straight," he said. "Does Mario have to work for the money as punishment—or does he just have to get it somewhere?" "He just has to get it," said Chester.

The teacher rereads a line spoken by Harry Cat, "Does Mario have to work for the money as punishment—or does he just have to get it somewhere?" She then poses a Narrative Query drawing attention to the character traits of Harry Cat: "Given what the author's already told us about Harry, what do you think he's up to?" Darleen responds:

> Darleen: I think that Harry, while he's talking that there's you know, those air bubbles? I think he's like, thinking of one of those. He's thinking that he can go, since he's a cat and he can go around other places and out in the subway station and get those two dollars and bring it back and send it somewhere so Mario can get it, and so Chester can get out."

TABLE 3 EXAMPLES OF QUERIES: INITIATING, FOLLOW-UP, AND NARRATIVE

Initiating Queries
- What is the author trying to say here?
- What is the author's message?
- What is the author talking about?

Follow-up Queries
- What does the author mean here?
- Did the author explain this clearly?
- Does this make sense with what the author told us before?
- How does this connect with what the author has told us here?
- Does the author tell us why?
- Why do you think the author tells us this now?

Narrative Queries
- How do things look for this character now?
- How has the author let you know that something has changed?
- How has the author settled this for us?
- Given what the author has already told us about this character, what do you think he's up to?

Darleen is able to connect knowledge of a character to her awareness of the plot and where it is going.

In summary, additional Queries help address the unique features of narratives. The Queries developed for QtA work for both expository and narrative texts, but some additional Queries for narratives can be useful. Table 3 on the previous page summarizes the examples of Initiating, Follow-up, and Narrative Queries that have been discussed in the previous sections.

RECAPPING QUERIES

In this chapter, we have described, explained, and demonstrated the characteristics, purposes, and effects of Queries. We also tried to demonstrate how Queries differ from traditional questions and how Queries can support students in building an understanding of text ideas.

CHAPTER 3

PLANNING

This chapter describes how teachers who use Questioning the Author (QtA) plan their lessons by approaching planning and decision making differently from more traditional lesson planning. To plan a lesson, some teachers rely on their teacher's manuals to identify the major ideas and information in a text and the kinds of questions and activities to use after reading it. An unfortunate consequence of relying on teacher's manuals is that teachers rarely scrutinize the text material themselves. The work already has been done, and the teachers generally trust that it has been done well. Other teachers plan by looking over the text and making their own decisions about what to teach. However, many of these teachers view the text as basically comprehensible and authors as infallible. Consequently, these teachers approach the text mainly to find the ideas students will be held accountable for recalling.

Although it seems reasonable to view teacher's manuals as reliable resources for content and instructional expertise, in many cases we have found that they do not measure up to such expectations. In many cases the identification of important content has not been done well, and the suggested questions fail to tap real understanding (Beck & McKeown, 1981). As we discussed in Chapters 1 and 2, the texts students are expected to read can be very dense and difficult for young learners to understand (Beck, McKeown, & Gromoll, 1989). Yet, in planning a lesson, there is often not enough recognition of the hard work it may take on the part of young readers to comprehend these texts that are used. QtA addresses these issues by encouraging teachers to adopt a new way to plan lessons, a way that involves teachers in trying to anticipate problems students might encounter when reading a text and the support they can offer to help students.

The relation between planning and teaching is different in QtA than it is in traditional teaching. Planning a lesson in QtA might be likened to a rehearsal in a stage production. In a rehearsal for a play, performers and directors do more than prepare or plan for the performance; they go a step beyond planning and play out how the performance will unfold. They block out scenes, determine what specific moves are most effective, and practice orchestrating the simultaneous demands of on-stage movements and cues from one another. A director's job is to anticipate audience response and reaction, decide what will enhance the production's overall appreciation and success, and prepare for potential problems.

In the same way that rehearsals are related to productions, planning a QtA lesson is related to teaching a QtA lesson. However, in a QtA lesson, the teacher is both the director and an actor. As the director, the teacher blocks out what will be discussed in the lesson and tries to anticipate how the lesson might develop. As an actor, the teacher must be ready to improvise as the lesson develops in ways he or she may not have anticipated.

Preparing a QtA lesson, in which teachers will not only direct but also participate as actors, calls for a special approach to planning. A key feature in effective planning is for the teacher to read the text that will be discussed in class while thinking about how the ideas in the text might be encountered by a young less skilled reader. We have found that taking the role of the student helps teachers better facilitate student efforts to construct meaning from a text. With this orientation in mind, we will consider the three QtA goals in planning.

GOALS OF PLANNING

IDENTIFYING MAJOR UNDERSTANDINGS AND POTENTIAL PROBLEMS

Planning for a QtA lesson always begins with a close reading of the text. The purpose of a close reading is more than just to become familiar with the content of the text, as in traditional planning. First, a teacher using QtA reads to determine the major understandings that students are to construct. Second, the teacher reads to anticipate and plan for potential problems in a text, such as lack of clarity or coherence and density of information that may impede understanding.

At first, the difference between becoming familiar with a text and determining major understandings may not seem obvious, but there is an important distinction. When preparing for a traditional lesson, teachers usually do not consider an author's intent or meaning. Most of the time, the author is in the background and the content of a text is in the foreground. The text is considered to be a source of fixed or constructed information or, in the case of narrative, a story that has already unfolded. Some teachers think of text as a finished product, a place to find meaning that already has been determined. With the author in the background, the text, as the author's attempt to present ideas and to invite readers to consider what those ideas mean, is also in the background.

QtA's emphasis on author awareness helps students and teachers bring the author to the foreground. When the author is a participant in the discussion, reading becomes a more active and interactive experience, more like a conversation. When, for example, we speak to our friends, argue a point, or even tell a story, our listener can interrupt, pose a question, or ask to have something clarified. In conversation, meaning is constructed immediately, with the assistance of the person communicating the ideas.

The conversation analogy may help capture the difference between two types of reading: reading to become familiar with what is in a text, and reading as if an author were there to question. In QtA, we teach students that the author is there to question. In their planning of a lesson, teachers read the text as a reader having a conversation with an author. The purpose of the conversation is to determine the major points the author is presenting and which of those are most important for students to understand.

Teachers also read to anticipate problems the text might pose to young and less experienced readers. As adult skilled readers, we usually do not have problems comprehending a text, even when the text is poorly written. We are skilled at making inferences about ideas not explicitly stated and making connections to previously read or known information. Teachers do these things automatically, which makes it harder to predict places in a text that students may find difficult or confusing. Yet, in order to be able to anticipate and plan for problematic portions of a text, teachers need to predict where students are most likely to have trouble.

One way for teachers to develop this awareness is to read the text and consciously monitor their comprehension processes, noticing when they are doing extra work. Extra work could include having to reread a portion of text to understand a passage or stopping to think about how one idea follows another. Teachers who find themselves doing extra work when they read can be reasonably sure that their students also will encounter difficulties and may not be able to resolve the problems without support.

In the next section, we present an example of planning using the text excerpt "How Pennsylvania Was Formed," a section from a social studies textbook (Silver Burdett & Ginn, 1990, p. 18). When reading the following excerpt, consider the kinds of understandings that we would want students to construct from this text. (The asterisks in the excerpt indicate text segments, which we will deal with shortly.)

> The shape of the land in North America has changed over millions of years. * About a million years ago, the earth got cooler. The winters were longer. A large amount of snow fell. Because the temperatures stayed cold, the snow did not melt. It got deeper and deeper. Slowly the snow grew into thick sheets of ice. These sheets are called glaciers. Some were over 2 miles (3 km) thick. Because of their great weight, the glaciers began to push south from the area around the North Pole. Some came as far south as Pennsylvania.*
>
> Glaciers move about 300 feet (91 m) a year. They push earth in front of them like giant bulldozers. The land was changed as the glaciers passed over it. * A mixture of sand, earth, rock, and stones was carried by the glaciers. This mixture is known as drift. In some places the drift formed long strips of raised land called ridges. A ridge made by drift is called a moraine. * But only some of the ridges on the land were pushed up out of the earth. * Some of the ridges were worn down by rain and wind.

The teacher who planned a QtA lesson using this text decided that the major understanding for students to construct is that glaciers are huge ice sheets that are largely responsible for forming the shape of the land in North America. An important issue to consider is that development of this understanding does not mean having students recite this statement. Rather, it means having students understand what is implied by the statement: how the shape and weight of glaciers could have been responsible for raising mountains and carving valleys.

The key text phrases in which the author provides information relating to the major point include the following: "slowly the snow grew into thick sheets of ice...called glaciers... which began to push south...as far south as Pennsylvania... and the land was changed as glaciers passed over it." When these phrases are combined, they create a summary statement of the major point. That is, the author establishes that glaciers caused various landforms.

There are several problems that young students might have in comprehending this text. One problem is that many terms are introduced that may make it difficult for students to grasp the main concept without getting distracted by the details. The author introduces terms such as *glaciers*, *drift*, *ridges*, and *moraine* in just a few sentences. The text becomes confusing as it moves from one new term to the next: "These sheets are called <u>glaciers</u>...sand, earth, rock, and stone...this mixture is known as <u>drift</u>...drift formed...<u>ridges</u>....A ridge made by drifts is called a <u>moraine</u>." These terms can be confusing because of their similarity and unfamiliarity to students. And, if students focus on the definitions of the terms, then they may not have enough attention left to grasp the main concept.

This example illustrates a typical problem with expository texts and the way they are treated in instruction. Students are often barraged with unfamiliar labels, terms, and technical language in expository text. Further, these terms are often emphasized by the way they are presented in the text. For example, notice that the words *glaciers*, *drift*, *ridges*, and *moraine* are underlined in the Pennsylvania text. Students may think that the terms are where their attention should be focused. In fact, this is the type of information they are typically asked to respond to in traditional questions and tests.

Yet, an accumulation of such terms and their meanings may not provide a deep understanding of the underlying concepts of the content they are supposed to be studying.

SEGMENTING TEXT

After reading the Pennsylvania text, identifying the major understanding we want students to build, and making some decisions about anticipated areas of difficulty, we are ready to think about segmenting the text. As mentioned earlier, segmenting means determining where to stop reading to initiate and develop discussion toward construction of meaning. In segmenting, it is the major understandings we want students to construct that drive decisions about where to stop reading and start discussion, not paragraph breaks in a text or where the text ends on a page. Sometimes a single sentence needs attention because the information it presents is key in constructing meaning. In other cases, a series of paragraphs can be dealt with all at once because there is no important material in the paragraphs or because the paragraphs are all about the same idea.

The important understanding in the text about Pennsylvania is that glaciers are responsible for the shape of the land. With this understanding as the instructional goal, the teacher determined that the first segment should include the material up to the first asterisk, which is just the first sentence, "The shape of the land in North America has changed over millions of years." This statement presents the main concept; however, because it is expressed rather incidentally, students may miss the point if it is not given emphasis.

The next stopping point, or the second segment, ends at the second asterisk. This text begins with "About a million years ago" and ends at the end of the first paragraph with "Some came as far south as Pennsylvania." The sentences in this segment all relate to the concept of glaciers.

The third segment is "Glaciers move about 300 feet (91m) a year. They push earth in front of them like giant bulldozers. The land was changed as the glaciers passed over it." In this portion of the text, the author introduces the idea that glaciers move and that this movement is what affects the shape of the land. This information is necessary to understand how glaciers change the land.

The fourth segment begins with "A mixture of sand" and ends with "is called a moraine," at the fourth asterisk. In this segment, the terms *drift*, *ridges*, and *moraine* are introduced. The teacher decided to stop here because the text gets more complicated with definitions and characteristics of the terms that are difficult themselves and also difficult to connect to the major theme.

The teacher decided that the final two sentences would be treated as two separate segments, as indicated by the fifth and sixth asterisks because each presents a qualifying feature of ridges. The teacher reasoned that if students read these sentences together, they could get confused easily.

After a teacher has decided on the major understandings students will construct and where to segment the text accordingly, the next step is to develop Queries.

DEVELOPING QUERIES

As discussed in Chapter 2, in planning Queries for a text, a teacher develops Initiating Queries to launch discussion, anticipates how students might respond, and develops potential Follow-up Queries to help focus and move the discussion. The teacher using the QtA approach developed Queries for the "How Pennsylvania Was Formed" text based on the six segments of the text.

After reading the first text segment, which refers to the main point of the changing shape of the land, the teacher wanted to know what students understood about the shape of the land. Her Initiating Query focused on that idea: "What do you think the author is telling us?" The teacher anticipated building on students' responses to establish the idea that landforms such as mountains and plateaus may not have always been as we now know them. In case students did not get the point, the teacher was prepared to ask a Follow-up Query such as the following, which would help students recall some of the basic geographical terms they had studied earlier: "What did the author tell us in the first chapter about the kind of shapes land can have?"

The second segment developed the concept of glaciers. The teacher planned to use an Initiating Query that could help students establish what glaciers are and provide a foundation for the discussion of a glacier's role in changing the land, such as, "What is the author telling us about snow, and ice, and glaciers?" The teacher wanted students to understand that glaciers are ice sheets of such enormous size that their weight forces them to move. However, the teacher anticipated that students might respond by saying simply that glaciers are ice sheets that move without referring to their enormous size and the connection between weight and movement. To address this situation, the teacher was prepared to ask a Follow-up Query to bring attention to this connection, such as, "So these sheets of ice started moving— does that make sense?"

The next segment continues to focus on the movement of glaciers and introduces how the movement affected the land:

> Glaciers move about 300 feet (91 m) a year. They push earth in front of them like giant bulldozers. The land was changed as the glaciers passed over it.

The teacher decided to begin with a general Query to find out if students could determine the consequence of glacial movement: "So *now* what does the author want us to know about glaciers?" The teacher planned a Follow-up Query to focus more directly on the notion that the glaciers changed the shape of the land. She decided that this might be ac-

complished by prompting students to connect glacial movement to the text's first sentence about the change in the
shape of land over millions of years, as follows: "How does
that connect to what the author already told us?"

The next text segment presents a lot of new information
and new terms, as mentioned:

> A mixture of sand, earth, rock, and stones was carried by the
> glaciers. This mixture is known as <u>drift</u>. In some places the drift
> formed long strips of raised land called <u>ridges</u>. A ridge made
> by drift is called a <u>moraine</u>.

The teacher's goal after reading this segment was to help
students sort out and summarize the information about how
glaciers move and how the new terms *drift*, *ridges*, and
moraine fit in. The Query she developed intended to signal
students that there is a lot to deal with and that the overall
picture is most important rather than the separate definitions
of the terms themselves: "Oh, boy, we've got some terms
piling up here—*drift, ridges, moraine*—what's that all about?"

The last two segments are qualifying statements about
ridges. The first of these states, "But only some of the ridges
were pushed up out of the earth." The teacher developed a
Query to signal students that they would have to work to
make sense of the statement and hinted that they would
need to think about what the author had said so far that
might make the statement confusing. The Query asked, "This
is really getting confusing. *Now* what has the author said?"

The final segment is the sentence "Some of the ridges
were worn down by rain and wind." The teacher planned to
use the following Query: "Now what is the author telling us
can happen?" By phrasing the Query in this way, the teacher
intended to indicate to the students that the information in
the sentence relates to something the author had already
talked about. The students would have read that ridges are
formed by glaciers, and now they should see that some
ridges are further affected by elements other than glaciers.

PLANNING FOR CONSTRUCTING MEANING

We have presented planning by discussing three goals: identifying important text ideas and anticipating problems students may have as they try to understand those ideas, segmenting text based on understandings and potential problems, and designing Queries to help students construct meaning from the text. However, we do not want our presentation to be misleading. Planning for a QtA lesson is not a three-step process; it is simply easier to introduce planning by dealing with the three considerations that need to be taken into account when planning. What we presented as three separate goals are all in service of one goal: helping students construct meaning from text. Achieving this goal involves making different kinds of decisions.

PLANNING A QtA LESSON FOR AN EXPOSITORY TEXT

In this section, we describe how a teacher using the QtA approach planned a lesson for an expository text. The excerpt used in this lesson plan is titled "Early Eskimo Life" and is from a social studies textbook (Laidlaw, 1985, pp. 68–72). Before this excerpt, the text presents information about the climate, culture, and geography of Alaska. The text in "Early Eskimo Life" describes the Eskimo people, their food, clothing, shelters, and transportation. While reading the following excerpt, consider the kinds of understandings that we would want students to construct from the text. (The segments created by the teacher are indicated by asterisks.)

Early Eskimo Life

Group life of the early Eskimos. Eskimos generally lived together in groups. A group of Eskimos might have had as many as several hundred people. Other groups might have been made up of just one family. These smaller family groups might have had around twenty people in them. These groups were

---

made up of grandparents and married sons and their families. An important reason why Eskimos lived in groups was to share work. The Eskimos had to fill their own needs for food, clothing, and housing. It was much easier to fill these needs if everyone had a certain job to do. Working together helped the Eskimos live in the cold climate of the tundra region. *

Food for the Eskimos. The early Eskimos depended on animals to fill most of their needs. It was from animals that the Eskimos got most of their food. Caribou meat and seal meat were their favorite foods. The Eskimos also ate meat from polar bears, from a kind of oxen, and from birds.

The Eskimos got some of their food from the Alaskan waters. During the summer months they caught many kinds of fish. The Eskimos worked in large groups to hunt whales. The Eskimos used a kind of long spear called a <u>harpoon</u> to catch whales. *

There were a few plants on the tundra that the Eskimos used for food. They ate the roots, stem, and berries of certain plants. However, the Eskimos could not depend on plants to fill their need for food. *

Clothing from animal skins. The Eskimos made their clothing from animal skins. Their first choice was the skins of caribou. These skins were warm but lightweight. The Eskimos also used the skins of polar bears, Arctic foxes, and seals to make clothing. Since sealskin is waterproof, the Eskimos also used it for the bottoms of their boots. * In winter the Eskimos wore two suits of clothing. Each suit had pants, mittens, and fur-lined stockings. Each suit also had a fur parka—a jacket with a hood. In summer the Eskimos wore only one suit of clothing.

Eskimo shelters. There are some people who think that the Eskimos lived only in snow houses called <u>igloos</u>. In fact, however, the Eskimos used this word as their name for different kinds of houses. * Most Eskimos built snow houses to live in only for a short time. They often lived in snow houses while they hunted animals.

The Eskimos built different kinds of houses for winter and for summer. They generally lived in sod houses in winter. Sod houses became very damp in the summer. So most Eskimos lived in tents during the summer months. The tents were made from the skins of animals such as caribou or seals. The skins

---

were stretched over whalebone poles. The Eskimos were able to take apart and roll up these summer houses. *

Transportation of the Eskimos. Because the Eskimos hunted to fill their needs, they moved fairly often. They went over ice, snow, water, and land in search of animals. * The Eskimos used several different kinds of <u>transportation</u>—a means of carrying people and goods from place to place.

In winter the Eskimos used sleds to go over the snow and ice. Dogs were used to pull the sleds. In summer the Eskimos sometimes walked from place to place. They also used boats. They used a small boat called a <u>kayak</u>, which generally held only one person. They also used a larger boat called an <u>umiak</u>. This kind of boat was large enough to haul belongings or to use in hunting whales. Both kinds of boats had a wooden frame covered with sealskin.

The teacher who used the QtA approach to teach this text decided that the major understanding she wanted her students to construct was that the early Eskimos had to depend on one another and their environmental resources for food and survival. In particular, Eskimos had to depend on animals for food, clothing, shelter, and transportation. The goal was not to have students state the concept but rather to have them build an understanding of what it means to be completely dependent on the environment. The text provides evidence that promoting this understanding also was the author's major goal because it contains multiple references to how the Eskimos lived in groups and hunted for food, such as, "Eskimos generally lived together in groups...to share work...to fill their own needs for food, clothing, and housing.... [They] depended on animals...[for] most of their food.... Caribou meat and seal meat were their favorite foods...also... polar bears...oxen, and birds...[They] worked in large groups to hunt whales.... Because the Eskimos hunted to fill their needs, they moved fairly often." These key phrases, taken together, establish the point that the Eskimos depended on environmental resources for their survival. However, we want to emphasize that the point was not to have students remember these phrases as disconnected pieces of information about Eskimos. Rather, the point of the lesson was to prompt students to use the information to develop an understanding of how the Eskimos were able to depend on their environment.

One problem that the teacher thought some students would have while trying to build an understanding of Eskimos' dependency on their environment is that all the pieces of information in the text seem to be treated equally. This may make it hard for a young reader to sort out important from less important information. Information that is relatively insignificant seems to get the same attention as something more directly connected to the major concept of the text. Some key text phrases illustrate why this may be a problem. For example, the author describes layers of clothing in a somewhat lengthy and detailed way, stating that "caribou skins...were warm but lightweight" and that "sealskin is waterproof" and explaining that the winter suits had "pants, mittens, and fur-lined stockings." This portion of text represents the author's attempt to exemplify and elaborate on a point that he has already made: Eskimos depend as much on animals to provide the major source of clothing as they do for everything else mentioned. Yet, this point is not expressed clearly. What may be more memorable for students are the details of the Eskimos' wardrobe.

Later, in the section of the text on transportation, the author makes an important point rather incidentally. He mentions the defining characteristic of the Eskimos' lifestyle that illustrates their environmental dependency: they had to follow the animals they hunted. The statement "Because the Eskimos hunted to fill their needs, they moved fairly often" introduces for the first time a very important idea about the nature of the Eskimo existence that is only alluded to earlier in the text. Eskimos had to follow the animals because the climate made it difficult to depend on plants and other sources of food. Although this is an important point, the author does not present it clearly. Instead, the author mentions rather incidentally that the Eskimos hunt and move, then he ends the topic. So, although it is an important piece of information that connects directly to an understanding that we want students to construct, it gets little attention in the text.

Because equal attention is given to both more and less important pieces of information in the text, students may have difficulty sorting out what is important. The tendency may be for students to get caught up in unrelated and scattered details about the Eskimos and not to see how the ideas support the major understanding about how Eskimos had to live. Students could finish reading this text without constructing meaning of the most important concept unless the teacher prepares well to prevent this from happening.

The teacher using QtA segmented the "Early Eskimo Life" text based on the lesson goal to construct understanding and the possible problems that might interfere with achieving it. The first segment of text included the whole section "Group life of the early Eskimos" (before the first asterisk) because it introduces and exemplifies the major understanding, that Eskimos depend on their environment and one another to fill their needs. The teacher decided to use the following Query to set the discussion in motion: "What has the author told us about the Eskimos' life?"

If students did not mention the main theme, the teacher planned the Follow-up Query "What does the author mean by 'the Eskimos had to fill their own needs'?" Another Follow-up Query that might be useful to connect the details of Eskimo life with the main concept presented is "How does filling their own needs connect to the other things the author told us about in this section?"

Next, the teacher decided to read the first two paragraphs in the "Food for the Eskimos" section. She viewed these two paragraphs as a segment because they describe the animals the Eskimos used for food. Thus, the paragraphs could help students understand the Eskimos' dependency on animals in their environment. To begin discussion of this segment, the teacher intended to use the Query "What's the author telling us about the Eskimos' food?"

Because the text names the many kinds of animals the Eskimos used for food, the author seems to suggest that these particular animals were eaten because they were available in the environment. If the discussion did not bring out these points, the teacher anticipated using Follow-up Queries such as

- The author has given many examples of animals that the Eskimos eat. How does this connect to what the author already told us about how the Eskimos live?

- Let's see, we've got caribou, seals, polar bears, and fish —what's so special about these animals? Why would the Eskimos eat *them*?

For the next segment, the teacher decided to read the last paragraph in the section "Food for the Eskimos." The implicit message here is that it is too cold to raise crops on the tundra; therefore, once the Eskimos used all the plants that grew in the wild, they would not be able to reproduce them. Such an inference probably would not be easy for students to make, so the teacher decided that she would treat this paragraph, as follows, separately:

> There were a few plants on the tundra that the Eskimos used for food. They ate the roots, stem, and berries of certain plants. However, the Eskimos could not depend on plants to fill their need for food.

To assist students in making an inference about the effects of climate on the Eskimos' diet, the teacher decided to use the Query "What does the author mean by 'the Eskimos could not depend on plants to fill their needs'?"

The teacher anticipated that students might respond by simply saying that it is too cold for plants to grow on the tundra. To prompt students to explain this connection further, she planned to ask the Follow-up Query "Does that make sense here?"

The next segment the teacher created was the first paragraph of the "Clothing from animal skins" section. The teacher chose to read only this one paragraph in the section because it relates directly to how the Eskimos used and depended on their environment, whereas the second paragraph presents some irrelevant details of the Eskimo wardrobe, which could distract student attention from the main point. The teacher planned to begin with a Query to, again, get at the idea that Eskimos use the animals in their environment such as "What's the author trying to tell us about the Eskimos' clothing?"

Another goal that the teacher had for this segment was to draw students' attention to the notion that, although caribou was the Eskimos' first choice for clothing, they sometimes used other animals. This information could reinforce the ideas that the Eskimos had to use what was available, and caribou may not always have been available. The Query the teacher used for this purpose was as follows:

The author tells us that caribou was the Eskimos' first choice to make clothing from, yet they used a lot of other animals, too. What do you think that means?

The next segment includes the second paragraph in the "Clothing from animal skins" section and the first two sentences in the "Eskimo shelters" section. The decision was made to continue reading past the second paragraph from the clothing section because this section did not include any information the teacher wanted to draw attention to. The teacher chose to stop after the first two sentences in the shelters section, which deals with the meaning of *igloo*, because she wanted to clarify how Eskimos used the word *igloo*. The author says that *igloo* refers to all kinds of houses but then continues to talk about only snow houses for the rest of the paragraph. For this segment, the teacher planned the following Query to help establish that *igloo* refers to many kinds of houses before students read on about the stereotypical igloos: "What is the author telling us about this word *igloo*?"

Next, the teacher planned to read the rest of the section on housing, which includes the following material:

> Most Eskimos built snow houses to live in only for a short time. They often lived in snow houses while they hunted animals.
>
> The Eskimos built different kinds of houses for winter and for summer. They generally lived in sod houses in winter. Sod houses became very damp in the summer. So most Eskimos lived in tents during the summer months. The tents were made from the skins of animals such as caribou or seals. The skins were stretched over whalebone poles. The Eskimos were able to take apart and roll up these summer houses.

The teacher planned to launch discussion by first signaling that there is a lot of information in this segment and posing a Query to help students deal with it:

> Let's try to sort out this information about Eskimos' houses. What is the author telling us about all these different kinds of houses?

The teacher then planned to work with students' responses to the Query to establish that Eskimo housing was not permanent, but that Eskimos built different kinds of shelters to fit the climate and to allow them to move easily. The need for easy movement may not be clear to students at this point because the text only alludes to the Eskimos' nomadic lifestyle in the first two sentences of this segment with the information that Eskimos "built snow houses to live in only for a short time" and "often lived in snow houses while they hunted animals."

The teacher planned to read the first two sentences of the transportation section as the next segment. In this short segment, the author finally makes explicit the characteristic feature of the early Eskimos' lifestyle—they had to move around to hunt the animals they depended on to fill their needs:

> **Transportation of the Eskimos.** Because the Eskimos hunted to fill their needs, they moved fairly often. They went over ice, snow, water, and land in search of animals.

The teacher planned to begin with the following Query: "What is the author telling us here?" She anticipated following up with Queries such as these:

- What does it mean that they moved fairly often?
- How does this connect with searching for animals?
- How do these ideas connect with what the author told us earlier about the Eskimos' houses?

The rest of the passage about transportation was selected as the final segment. Here, the teacher planned not to pay attention to the details about types of transportation but to focus on the main concept about the early Eskimos' need to live as nomads in order to garner the resources necessary to survive. She posed the Query "How does this connect to what we learned about the Eskimos' lifestyle?"

The segments and Queries detailed in this section illustrate how one teacher developed and maintained a focus on the major concept in an expository text. The teacher kept this focus even though the information relating to this concept is often implicit rather than explicit and is scattered throughout the text interspersed with less relevant details.

PLANNING A QtA LESSON FOR NARRATIVE TEXT

Recall that when we discussed developing Queries for narrative and expository texts in Chapter 2, we listed some of the special features of narrative texts, such as the author's style and elements of plot and character development. However, despite a few additional considerations, the goals of planning to read narratives with a QtA approach are the same as those for expository texts.

The following example details how one teacher planned a QtA lesson using the fable "The Fox and the Crow," from a teaching resource for a language arts program (Silver Burdett & Ginn, 1989). The fable is about a conceited young crow and a very sly fox. Both of these characters are introduced at the beginning of the story. Then, in the next part, the fox doles out his flattery to the crow. Finally, the crow falls victim to the fox's praise and her own conceit. Because of the crow's conceited attitude, the fox is able to trick her into dropping a piece of meat that she has stolen. While reading the following story, consider how the text could be segmented and what Queries could be used to direct students to the main themes. (As in the previous excerpt, the text segments created by the teacher are indicated by asterisks.)

The Fox and the Crow

The cawing of crows filled the air as they swept across the pink sky swooping to and fro in a black cloud towards their untidy homes in the treetops.

They were led by an old and graying bird whose word was law, and behind him came the other older members of the family, who in turn were followed by the younger crows who had been hatched in the spring. These were impatient young birds, proud of their strong young wings and throaty voices. * Lagging far behind them, apart from the others, was the most conceited young crow of all.

She had no need to hurry because she was confident that she could easily catch up whenever she wanted. As her wings flapped lazily in the evening sky her bright eyes spotted the open window of a house below her and she decided to investigate. *

Swooping past the window, she was delighted to see a table in the room beyond laden with delicious food. Turning awkwardly, she looped backwards, flew down and through the open window and snatched up a large piece of beef. Her heart beating with excitement, she flew with her prize to a small clump of fir trees standing nearby. The meat was heavy, and breathlessly she settled on a comfortable branch, her bright eyes sparkling with satisfaction and greed. *

A dying sunbeam glanced through the branches and settled on something brown and furry among the pine needles and bracken at the foot of the tree. The brown patch moved silently forward and there, in the rays of the setting sun, was a fox.

It was rather early for him to be setting out for his night's hunting, but he was very hungry after sleeping for most of the day. When he looked up and saw the crow with the juicy piece of meat in her mouth, his mouth watered with envy. * The crow glanced down at him with scorn. She thought the fox a rather common form of creature. Why, he could not even fly! *

The fox concentrated his gaze upon the meat, his brain working quickly, his amber eyes alive and bright. At all costs, he decided, he must have the meat. His beautiful brush-like tail swayed gently and his tongue flicked over his jaws. Then he smiled up at the crow and said in a soft voice, "What vision of beauty is this that I see?" The crow cocked her head on one side and stared downward still holding the piece of meat firmly in her beak. Then she heard the fox say, "Surely those beautiful wings must have come from a fairy nest, they are so fine and strong! And those eyes, so soft and liquid to behold, so starlike and so gentle...." The crow fidgeted a little and thought, "Perhaps I was mistaken. The fox appears to be a most elegant and sensible fellow." * The fox took a breath and went on: "Never in all my travels have I seen such exquisite poise, such dignity. And such form! Surely even the graceful swans on the lake would be green with envy if they could see such soft and fairy-like lightness!"

The crow preened herself but still held tightly to her prize. She was longing to hear more and waited expectantly. The fox continued, "That smooth beak, those dainty feet. This must be the wonderful crow that I have heard so much about." The crow took one step to the right and one to the left but still held on to the meat.* Then the fox muttered, "Now, if only she could sing like the nightingales! But of course, with such outward beauty she probably cannot sing at all. What a pity!" The fox sighed, "If only she could sing she would be the queen of them all." *

The conceited crow could contain herself no longer. The fox, she decided, was a gentleman of taste and quality. She must show him that her voice was every bit as beautiful as her figure and coloring. She simply could not remain silent any longer, and she opened her beak as wide as possible. "CAW! CAW! CAW!" she croaked, making the most ugly sound that ever was heard.

There was a sudden bark of excitement from the foot of the tree as the slice of juicy meat fell onto the ground. The fox pounced upon it instantly and gripped it between his strong jaws. As he ran off the crow screamed in fury, "CAW! CAW! CAW! You wicked thief! Give me back my meat. CAW! CAW! You wicked thief!" But the fox did not return despite her pleas.

For "The Fox and the Crow," the teacher using QtA decided that the major understanding for students to grasp is that the outcome of this fable is ironic. The irony is that the crow's conceit about the superiority of her own qualities makes her vulnerable and results in the loss of something she prizes. At the root of her conceit is that she cannot see herself as she really is or see others as they really are.

The author reveals the young crow's conceited attitude in two key phrases. First, notice that the young crow is not in her appointed place in the flight hierarchy and that the word *conceited* is used to describe her: "Lagging far behind...was the most conceited young crow of all." Second, the author further describes the crow by stating, "She had no need to hurry because she was confident that she could easily catch up whenever she wanted."

Key phrases later in the story show how the author developed the point that the crow's conceit prevented her from seeing herself as she really is and from seeing others as they really are. For example, when the crow is stealing the meat, the author describes it in a way that conveys the crow's excitement and satisfaction: "her heart beating with excitement, she flew with her prize...sparkling with satisfaction." But in a later passage, when the fox steals the meat from the crow, the crow's attitude about stealing changes. She "screamed in fury" at the fox, calling him a "wicked thief." The contrast between these two incidents is an aspect of the irony in the story.

A potential problem in constructing meaning of the irony in "The Fox and the Crow" is that the author does not point out what is ironic, so readers have to discover it for themselves. It may be difficult for students to use details of specific incidents in the fable to come to an understanding of the irony. Therefore, the teacher can help students make the connections that will highlight the irony. Two phrases, "her eyes sparkling with satisfaction and greed" and "you wicked thief," clearly show the two different views the crow has about stealing. The difference may be missed by students if the two incidents are not contrasted.

Also, the sentences "She thought the fox a rather common form of creature," and "The crow fidgeted a little and thought, 'Perhaps I was mistaken. The fox appears to be a most elegant and sensible fellow'" show how the crow's conceited attitude provides the ironic foundation for her vulnerability. The fox's flattery can work only because of the crow's conceit, and so it is the crow's changing view of the fox that sets the stage for her being tricked.

Students probably will need help to understand the ironic consequences of the bird's conceited attitude. That is, her conceit eventually makes her all the more vulnerable to being the victim of the very crime she so confidently commits. This vulnerability connects to the success of the fox's strategy to flatter the crow in order to get the meat. All these connections are subtle and, therefore, will need special attention from the teacher. The teacher using QtA in this example determined that her students would need to be encouraged to think about how the fox's flattery changed the crow's original opinion of the fox, which resulted in defeating the crow at her own game.

After deciding what the major understandings are and where the potential problems might be to building understanding in this story, the teacher using QtA decided to include the first paragraph and part of the second in the first segment. She wanted to focus on the established crow hierarchy and the pride of the young crows, even though they are last in line:

> The cawing of crows filled the air as they swept across the pink sky swooping to and fro in a black cloud towards their untidy homes in the treetops.
> They were led by an old and graying bird whose word was law, and behind him came the other older members of the family, who in turn were followed by the younger crows who had been hatched in the spring. These were impatient young birds, proud of their strong young wings and throaty voices.

The teacher wanted to direct students' attention to the flying order so they could use the information to build an understanding of how things usually are, and use that as a basis for understanding the young crow's unusual behavior. Here is the Query she developed: "What has the author told us about the crows through the description of their flying order?"

In the second segment (the text before the second asterisk), the author describes the young crow as "the most conceited young crow of all." This statement presents very important information that students will need to know if the rest of the story is to make sense. The teacher planned to focus on information describing the crow, using either the first general Query presented following or the second more specifically focused one:

- What is the author telling us about this young crow?
- What is the author telling us about this crow when he says, "She had no reason to hurry," and "her wings flapped lazily"?

The third segment is as follows:

> Swooping past the window, she was delighted to see a table in the room beyond laden with delicious food. Turning awkwardly, she looped backwards, flew down and through the open window and snatched up a large piece of beef. Her heart beating with excitement, she flew with her prize to a small clump of fir

trees standing nearby. The meat was heavy, and breathlessly she settled on a comfortable branch, her bright eyes sparkling with satisfaction and greed.

Segmenting the text here allows the teacher to focus students' attention on what the crow does and how she feels about it so that they have that information available to use later to make a connection between the two different accounts of "stealing" that occur in the story. Again, the teacher planned two alternative Queries, one general and one more specific:

- So, what has the author told us in this paragraph?

- What has the author told us about how the crow feels about what she has done?

In the next segment, the author introduces a new character, the envious fox:

A dying sunbeam glanced through the branches and settled on something brown and furry among the pine needles and bracken at the foot of the tree. The brown patch moved silently forward and there, in the rays of the setting sun, was a fox.

It was rather early for him to be setting out for his night's hunting, but he was very hungry after sleeping for most of the day. When he looked up and saw the crow with the juicy piece of meat in her mouth, his mouth watered with envy.

The teacher planned the following Query to encourage students to think about the proud, conceited bird with the piece of meat in relation to the envious fox: "What picture has the author created for us now?"

The next segment is just a few sentences. These statements reveal in a direct way the crow's conceited attitude about herself and how her attitude influences her view of the fox: "The crow glanced down at him with scorn. She thought the fox a rather common form of creature. Why, he could not even fly!" The teacher decided to use the following

Query to encourage students to talk about the crow's conceited nature and connect it with the crow's reaction to the fox: "Based on what the author has already told us about the crow, why would she think the fox is a 'rather common form of creature'?" If students did not make the connection, the teacher planned to draw their attention to the last line, "Why he could not even fly!"

In the next segment the fox is trying to trick the crow into giving him the meat by flattering her:

> The fox concentrated his gaze upon the meat, his brain working quickly, his amber eyes alive and bright. At all costs, he decided, he must have the meat. His beautiful brush-like tail swayed gently and his tongue flicked over his jaws. Then he smiled up at the crow and said in a soft voice, "What vision of beauty is this that I see?" The crow cocked her head on one side and stared downward still holding the piece of meat firmly in her beak. Then she heard the fox say, "Surely those beautiful wings must have come from a fairy nest, they are so fine and strong! And those eyes, so soft and liquid to behold, so star-like and so gentle...." The crow fidgeted a little and thought, "Perhaps I was mistaken. The fox appears to be a most elegant and sensible fellow."

The teacher developed a Query that aimed to encourage students to think about the fox's plan rather than just what he said: "So, what is the fox up to here?"

In the next segment, the issue becomes how the fox's compliments are affecting the crow:

> The fox took a breath and went on: "Never in all my travels have I seen such exquisite poise, such dignity. And such form! Surely even the graceful swans on the lake would be green with envy if they could see such soft and fairy-like lightness!"
>
> The crow preened herself but still held tightly to her prize. She was longing to hear more and waited expectantly. The fox continued, "That smooth beak, those dainty feet. This must be the wonderful crow that I have heard so much about." The crow took one step to the right and one to the left but still held on to the meat.

Here, the teacher's goal was to pose the following Query that would help students focus on why the crow was so easily swayed: "So, *now* what does the crow think of the fox?" The teacher also decided to reinforce the connection between the crow's conceited nature and the effect of the flattery by asking the Query "What changed the crow's mind about the fox and how does that connect with what we already know about the crow?"

In the next segment, the reader discovers that the fox is going to trick the crow into dropping the meat by encouraging her to sing:

> Then the fox muttered, "Now, if only she could sing like the nightingales! But of course, with such outward beauty she probably cannot sing at all. What a pity!" The fox sighed, "If only she could sing she would be the queen of them all."

The teacher's goal in this segment was to encourage students to recognize the fox's intentions by discussing why the fox wants the crow to sing. The teacher planned to ask the following Query: "The author has already described the many compliments the fox gave to the crow. Now, the fox wants the crow to sing. Why might that be?"

In the last segment of this text, we find that the fox's trick has worked, and he ends up with the stolen piece of meat:

> The conceited crow could contain herself no longer. The fox, she decided, was a gentleman of taste and quality. She must show him that her voice was every bit as beautiful as her figure and coloring. She simply could not remain silent any longer, and she opened her beak as wide as possible. "CAW! CAW! CAW!" she croaked, making the most ugly sound that ever was heard.
>
> There was a sudden bark of excitement from the foot of the tree as the slice of juicy meat fell onto the ground. The fox pounced upon it instantly and gripped it between his strong jaws. As he ran off the crow screamed in fury, "CAW! CAW! CAW! You wicked thief! Give me back my meat. CAW! CAW! You wicked thief!" But the fox did not return despite her pleas.

Although this ending may not be difficult for the students to understand, the teacher decided to get discussion going by asking: "Wow, what do you think of that?"

Because this is a fable and because the story's irony is the major understanding that she wanted students to construct, the teacher decided to have students discuss a possible moral for the story. She decided to start off that part of the discussion as follows: "Hmm. The crow calls the fox a wicked thief. Do you think there's anything strange about that?"

This Query might encourage students to discuss the crow's remark and connect it to the crow's theft of the meat earlier in the story. This may lead to discussion about how the crow views herself and how she views the fox. If students need help to get to the broader understanding about how the crow's view of herself allowed the fox to trick her so easily, the teacher planned to use one more Query: "What does the crow think has happened?"

We hope these examples have expressed a sense of the planning process in QtA. They also should reinforce the notion of how decisions for segmenting and developing Queries for narrative text are driven by the major understandings of the story that the teacher wants students to construct.

RECAPPING PLANNING

There are three basic goals in planning a QtA text-based lesson, whether it is for expository or narrative text:

1. to identify the major understandings students should construct and to anticipate potential problems in the text
2. to segment the text to focus on information needed to build understandings
3. to develop Queries that promote the building of those understandings

Segmenting the text and developing Queries serve as mechanisms that help teachers to assist students in constructing meaning of the major understandings.

Finally, planning in QtA changes the roles and tasks of the teacher from what is more typical of traditional lesson planning. As we noted earlier, it might help to think that QtA planning is akin to a rehearsal for teaching. This rehearsal includes anticipating potential problems and responses of students.

CHAPTER 4

DISCUSSION

This chapter describes discussion from a Questioning the Author (QtA) perspective. Generally, discussion is associated with sharing ideas and talking between and among students. The problem is that for teachers, the word *discussion* may conjure up difficulties with classroom management and control combined with shortages of time, all of which may cloud perspectives about the possibilities for learning that come from engaging students in discussions. We begin this section as we have with the chapters on Queries and planning by contrasting QtA discussions and more traditional classroom discussions. Then, we describe features of QtA discussion and provide examples of the specific ways teachers can promote these features.

The primary purpose of a QtA discussion is to help students construct meaning, or build understanding, of text ideas that are initially encountered in the course of reading. And, as we have emphasized in the earlier chapters, constructing meaning during reading is key to understanding the purposes of a QtA discussion. During a QtA discussion, students do the work of thinking and building meaning as ideas are first encountered in a text. One way to conceptualize a QtA discussion is to imagine that, when students engage in reading and talking about a text, they enter a maze. The ideas in a text make up the maze, and the goal for working through it is to reach understanding. Students must follow any unexpected twists and turns the text-maze presents, recognize dead-ends, and use strategic maneuvers to get through. The QtA teacher has already been through the maze, so he or she knows what students are facing. However, the teacher's job is not to show students the path through the maze, but rather to assist them as they discover their own way through. In most mazes, there is more than one pathway to the goal. QtA helps students to navigate through a text, but it does not take away student responsibility for figuring out how to do it.

KEY COMPONENTS OF QtA DISCUSSION

The two key components of a QtA discussion are the teacher's role and student contributions. From a QtA perspective, the teacher's role involves participating in thinking and helping students develop ideas rather than managing thinking and explaining ideas. Student contributions involve collaborating with one another to construct ideas as they are encountered in a text rather than presenting ideas they have already constructed from a text.

In a QtA discussion, the teacher participates as a collaborator in thinking and building meaning. In order to do so, as we noted earlier, teachers attempt to develop a sense of a text similar to what a young reader might have. Teachers must spend time reading closely and considering the most important text ideas for students to construct. This initial work gives teachers a sense of where in the presentation students may most likely need some encouragement or other input from them. During a QtA discussion, teachers simultaneously balance two perspectives of the "maze": one is the student's perspective (a ground-level view) and the other is their own perspective (a bird's eye view). Teachers have to keep in mind that, to students, the text may first appear confusing, dense, and ambiguous. At the same time, teachers have to consider the major understandings they want students to construct and the actions they can take to help students get there. This means that during a QtA discussion, teachers have to coordinate dual perspectives. It is this coordination that changes a teacher's role from one who simply manages and explains to one who participates in and facilitates the kind of thinking needed to build understanding of ideas.

In the following section, we will consider how student contributions in a QtA discussion may differ from the kind of contributions they might make in a more traditional discussion.

COMPARING TRADITIONAL AND QtA DISCUSSIONS

Table 4 contrasts features of traditional and QtA discussions. As the table shows, in traditional discussions, students typically present ideas they have already constructed from a text. In contrast, in QtA discussions, students collaborate to construct ideas as they are encountered in a text.

WHAT STUDENTS DO IN THE TWO KINDS OF DISCUSSIONS

Perhaps one of the most typical patterns of traditional classroom discussions is that students tend to report infor-

TABLE 4 COMPARISON OF TRADITIONAL AND QUESTIONING THE AUTHOR DISCUSSIONS

Traditional Discussions

Students present ideas they have already constructed from a text.

Students:

• report information from a text.

• are engaged in shared retrieval of acquired facts and opinions; participation tends to be flat.

Teachers:

• treat various students' contributions equally. The goal seems to be to collect and validate all contributions with little apparent focus.

• dominate the thinking. They do most of the work of constructing ideas and signal students to merely react to the ideas they have constructed.

Questioning the Author Discussions

Students collaborate to construct ideas as they are encountered in a text.

Students:

• develop and connect ideas from a text.

• are engaged in shared investigation of meaning; participation tends to be active.

Teachers:

• differentiate among student contributions. The goal is to focus contributions toward building an understanding of text ideas.

• ignite and respond to student contributions strategically. They advance student thinking and signal students to take ideas further whenever possible.

mation from a text, information they have already distilled on their own. Because students are engaged in shared retrieval of acquired facts and opinions, participation may be flat. Although students may argue and debate a peer's conclusion, how those conclusions were reached or how meaning was constructed from the author's presentation of information in the text is rarely the focus or purpose of a traditional discussion. In contrast, students in a QtA discussion are expected and encouraged to develop, connect, and especially explain ideas from a text, not just report information. Students are engaged in shared investigation of meaning, not just shared retrieval of information and beliefs, so participation tends to be active.

WHAT TEACHERS DO IN THE TWO KINDS OF DISCUSSIONS

As shown in Table 4, in a traditional discussion, teachers tend to treat various student contributions equally. The goal seems to be to collect and validate contributions with little apparent focus. Student contributions are collected, one after another, and frequently all are given equal attention or assigned equal significance. The teacher's role is to initiate contributions and manage disagreement. In contrast, a teacher using QtA deliberately attempts to differentiate among student contributions, attending to and using those responses that will help develop ideas. The goal is to focus contributions toward building an understanding of text ideas. Teachers act to assist students in their own construction of meaning, supporting them in their efforts to build ideas, not just present ideas.

Finally, as noted in the table, teachers in traditional classroom discussions tend to dominate the thinking. They do most of the work of constructing ideas and signal students to react to the ideas that they (the teachers) have constructed. Students may react to the ideas the teacher has constructed, but merely reacting is a different and less cognitively challenging task for students than constructing ideas themselves. In contrast, teachers in a QtA discussion try to ignite and respond strategically to students' contributions. They advance student thinking and signal students to take ideas further whenever possible.

Queries remain the major tools for helping students navigate through a text to construct meaning. However, Queries themselves are not the navigators; teachers are. Queries are used to initiate the discussion and then to support students in their attempts to grapple with ideas. A QtA discussion, however, is more than just student responses to teacher Queries, so teachers need other tools to facilitate meaning construction in the context of a discussion.

In the next section, we present what we refer to as *discussion moves* and demonstrate how these moves can assist teachers in maintaining the flexibility and improvisational decision making that is required of QtA teachers.

DISCUSSION MOVES

Discussion moves are actions that teachers take to assist them in orchestrating student ideas and making improvisational decisions. We have identified six QtA discussion moves: marking, turning back, revoicing, modeling, annotating, and recapping. The purpose of these moves is to help teachers keep students engaged in the constructive work of building understanding. The moves are neither sequential nor prescriptive. Rather, they are ways that we have seen teachers keep discussion focused and productive. A description of each discussion move follows.

MARKING

Teachers use marking by responding to student comments in a way that draws attention to certain ideas. By

---

marking, a teacher signals to students that an idea is of particular importance to the discussion. As an example, consider a student comment that was made during a discussion of the War of 1812: "The United States declared war on Great Britain because they kept stopping American ships." Because this comment contains a key reason for the declaration of war, a point that had not been brought up in earlier comments, the teacher wanted to draw attention to it. The teacher marked the student's idea by paraphrasing it and adding strategic intonation, saying, "Oh, so Great Britain was actually *stopping* American ships." By marking the student's comment in this way the teacher attempted to focus on the seriousness of another country stopping American ships at sea, underscoring the connections between that action and the act of declaring war.

Another way teachers can mark an idea is by explicitly acknowledging its importance. For example, they can say something like "Good point. It's important to know that stopping ships was seen as such a terrible act that the United States declared war because Great Britain was doing this." Such statements allow students to hear directly from the teacher why a comment is valued.

TURNING BACK

The turning back discussion move is associated with two actions. First, turning back refers to turning responsibility back to students for thinking through and figuring out ideas. Second, turning back also refers to turning students' attention back to the text as a source for clarifying their thinking. An example of turning back responsibility to students can be seen in the following comments made in a discussion about the book *Ralph S. Mouse* by Beverly Cleary. The students had been reading about an incident that takes place when a boy named Ryan brings Ralph, his pet mouse, to school. To show how smart Ralph is, Ryan has Ralph find his way through a maze. When Ralph fails to run through the maze, a student named Brad calls Ralph dumb. Ryan and Brad start to fight, and Ralph's motorcycle is broken as a result. When Ralph complains, Ryan says that it is Ralph's own fault for not getting through the maze the way he was supposed to.

The teacher's Query about the incident attempted to focus on how everything had gone wrong for Ralph that day: "How are things going for Ralph right now?" A student responded, "Ralph wasn't feeling too good about what Brad said." The student comment was very limited in light of all the things that had befallen Ralph, so the teacher probed for elaboration, saying, "Is that the big issue for Ralph—what Brad said?" This kind of teacher response turns responsibility back to students and encourages them to reveal more of their thinking.

Another way we have seen teachers using QtA probe for elaboration involves expressing confusion and turning back to the students for clarification. For example, a teacher might ask, "Wait—if what's upsetting Ralph is what *Brad* said about him, why does Ralph keep talking about how unfair *Ryan* has been to him?" This kind of turning back can be effective for motivating students to consider how other information in the text relates to the ideas they have expressed.

Probing for elaboration is one purpose for using turning back. Another reason is to prompt students to make connections. For example, to encourage students to connect their ideas with the ideas in the text, a teacher might ask, "Does it make sense that Ralph would be upset after hearing what Brad had said about him?" This kind of turning back encourages students to get involved in reasoning about ideas that have already been presented in the text.

Similarly, turning back can be used to encourage students to connect their ideas with the ideas of other students. For example, a teacher might ask, "How does what Alice just said about Ralph's feelings connect to what David said about

Ralph and his relatives?" This type of turning back is intended to help students connect scattered concepts and draw seemingly unrelated or forgotten information together so they can construct understanding of larger ideas.

Whatever the specific purpose in using turning back to students as a discussion move, the goal is to turn the responsibility for thinking and grappling for understanding back to students and to help teachers avoid taking over the thinking.

The other form of the turning back discussion move is turning back to text. Sometimes students offer an idea or opinion that contradicts or does not take into account information in the text. For example, a student comment such as, "I think Ralph should just go back to the hotel and forget about being in school," does not take into account that Ralph had originally asked Ryan to take him to school because he could no longer stay at the hotel where Ryan's mother is the housekeeper. Instead of encouraging students to consider the comment, the teacher could turn them back to the text by asking, "But is going back to the hotel a real option for Ralph? What did the author tell us about why Ralph asked Ryan to take him to school in the first place?" By turning students back to the text, the teacher can reduce unproductive digressions that can take a discussion off track.

In some cases, turning back to text is a quick way to clear up confusion. For example, a student commented, "Maybe Ralph could just drive his motorcycle to find a new place." However, this comment is in conflict with information in the text about Ralph's motorcycle. The teacher responded, "What did the author tell us about Ralph's motorcycle that connects to Noreen's suggestion?" Going back to the text allowed students to see that Ralph's motorcycle is in such bad shape that a trip is not feasible.

Turning back to text is useful when students introduce unrelated ideas and argue points that have little to do with the major content under consideration, or when they debate an issue that can be easily clarified by what the author has explicitly presented. Directing students back to the text addresses young students' tendency to go off on tangents, introducing irrelevant information. When students are reminded to take account of the author's words and ideas, they can refocus their attention on the more important ideas, and the discussion can return to more productive construction of meaning.

Whether directed to students for elaboration of their comments or to text for students to take better account of what an author has said, the turning back discussion move promotes students taking responsibility for grasping ideas and resolving issues in contrast to having the teacher explain information to them.

REVOICING

Another discussion move is revoicing. By revoicing, we mean interpreting what students are struggling to express and rephrasing the ideas so that they can become part of the discussion. Revoicing is applying an "in other words" mechanism to assist students in expressing their own ideas and distilling from their comments the most important information or implicit ideas.

Following is an example of revoicing from a discussion in which a student was trying to describe early New World colonists' dependency on Native Americans. The student commented, "The way it was going, they weren't going to make it because they didn't do it on their own. They had to depend on the Indians." The teacher recognized that the student had brought up an important understanding, but it was not phrased very clearly. So, the teacher revoiced the comment: "It seems you are saying that because the settlers depended on Native Americans for food and didn't learn how to grow their own food, they were going to have a hard time surviving." This kind of revoicing clarifies and captures the essence of an idea and allows a student's unwieldy ideas to become part of the discussion. When student comments are made clearer and more concise, they can be used more easily by other students who can respond to and build on the revoiced comments to construct meaning.

The revoicing move has a similar function to marking. In both cases, the "thinking" work has already been done by students, and the moves are used to emphasize and set up ideas so they can become a part of a productive discussion. That is, ideas have already been constructed by students, and the teacher revoices or marks them to clarify or emphasize them and make them easier for other students to react to and build upon.

In addition to the set of three discussion moves just discussed, marking, turning back, and revoicing, there is another set of discussion moves, in which teachers bring themselves into the interaction more directly than in the previous set of moves. The three additional moves, modeling, annotating, and recapping, will be discussed following.

MODELING

An old Chinese proverb captures the intention of modeling: "Tell me, I will forget. Teach me, I might remember. Show me, I will understand." "Show me" is a major part of modeling and for centuries has been fundamentally integrated into apprenticeship environments such as novice carpenters who learn their craft by watching masters or medical interns who follow experienced physicians. Moreover, modeling enables children to learn many things about the roles they are expected to assume in their environment: how people act at the dinner table, how visitors are treated when they come to the house, how purchases are made in stores, and how books are borrowed in libraries.

Although telling and explaining are more prevalent than modeling in formal instruction, the notion of modeling is widely supported as an effective pedagogical device. For example, in an algebra class teachers often say, "OK, I looked at each side of the equal sign and saw that I could get rid of this x by subtracting it from both sides, so that is what I will do next."

There have been many recommendations to extend modeling to other content domains, including reading (see, for example, Duffy, Roehler, & Herrmann, 1988). But what is modeling in reading? Because the act of reading is invisible to others, modeling is an attempt to "make public" some of the processes in which readers engage in the course of reading. When teachers model some of the things they do as they read, they are trying to show students how their mind is actively interacting with the ideas in the text.

There are some tendencies that reduce the potential impact of modeling as a teaching strategy. For example, contrived attempts to predict an obvious event, such as "I think the wolf is going to blow the third little pig's house down," do little to reveal what is involved in working with subtle ideas to make a less-than-obvious prediction. This example points to a common problem relating to examples of teachers' modeling that we have seen; what gets modeled tends to be the obvious. It also highlights the contrived nature of some kinds of modeling.

In contrast to the problems associated with modeling, modeling that is potentially beneficial helps students see things in texts they might not have noticed and allows students to observe or "overhear" how an expert thinks through a complicated idea. Which parts or ideas in a text that a teacher chooses to model is determined by the text ideas the teacher thinks students might need help with and by the teacher's spontaneous reactions to text. Additionally, a teacher can model what he or she was thinking about an issue under discussion as a way to make a point that students seem unable to reach.

Following, we provide some examples of how teachers have used the modeling discussion move. The examples represent general categories of what teachers chose to model. The first three show how modeling was used to communicate several teachers' affective responses to text. The remaining examples present instances of teachers' modeling their process of trying to build an understanding of confusing text.

The following example of a teacher modeling her response to an author's language comes from a transcript of a QtA lesson in which the teacher enjoyed an author's play on words. When the students and she were discussing that part, the teacher said, "The author made me laugh when he said that the mouse was 'scared squeakless.' Scared squeakless. I've heard of people being scared *speechless*, so the author is kind of playing with us to say a mouse is scared squeakless." By sharing her response to the humor in the text, this teacher modeled her appreciation of the author's language without overanalyzing it.

The next example shows how a teacher brought attention to some exquisitely presented material by encouraging appreciation of what the author did and how it affected her as a reader. In the course of a ninth-grade class discussion of the beginning of *Great Expectations* in which the escaped convict is described, the teacher said,

> What a frightening man! Mmm, every time I read Dickens I find myself in awe of the effect his use of language has on me. Those sentence fragments, how effective.... A man soaked in water, and smothered in mud, and lamed by stones, and cut by flints, and stung by nettles, and torn by briars, who limped and shivered and glared and growled....

The teacher's repetition of text phrases emphasizes their cumulative effect on the reader. It also provides an opportunity for students to see how that effect is created.

Teachers' reactions can be brief, such as, "The author really made me feel how cold it was without even using the word *cold*, just by mentioning the way the students' breath made 'clouds' in the air and the way she describes them as being 'hidden under hats and scarves and sweaters'."

These three examples show how teachers exposed their own reactions about what an author said that evoked a particular response and why. None of the examples is particularly long or pedantic; rather, they seem to be natural attempts to share a response to the text.

Another way in which modeling can be used effectively is in identifying confusing portions of text and showing how a reader might work through them. Calling attention to text that is not clear is also an opportunity to reinforce the QtA emphasis on the fallible author, someone who is trying to communicate a message and who is sometimes not successful. In the example that follows, notice how a teacher modeled how a reader might handle a text that seems to present too many details:

> When I first read all this description about the features of the land, I thought, what's going on here? What's the author want me to remember from all the information? So I went back and read it again and decided that the big idea was that this was a good place to build a town because it was close to a river and protected by forests on the other side. That's what the author was trying to get at.

A teacher's modeling of grappling with portions of text that were somewhat contradictory went like this:

> OK now, when I was reading this, I understood that in the first sentence, the author said most people in developing countries make a living by farming. But later on the author said, "However, there is a shortage of food." Well, if everyone makes their living by farming, why would there be a shortage of food? What's going on here? Let's think this through.

Discussion

Additionally, in QtA, modeling can be an effective way to tell students what the teacher intended when it becomes obvious that students do not know. Consider the following instance, when a teacher initiated discussion about a story with an introduction that referred to animals who were carrying on a conversation. The teacher asked, "What do you think the author is telling us about the kind of story this is going to be?" The teacher wanted students to establish a fantasy framework for reading the story and expected them to respond to the idea that animals were talking and therefore it was a "pretend" story. The initial response to the teacher's Query was an array of blank faces. Rewordings of the Query only succeeded in eliciting that the story was fiction, and no student was able to elaborate on that response. At that point, the teacher stepped in and modeled how she had responded to the introduction. She said, "When I read this I thought, 'We've got a mouse and a cricket talking to each other here, so I know this story is going to be a kind of fantasy'."

The teacher's decision to model was much better than deciding to continue asking the same Query. By providing the explanation couched in terms of her own thinking, the teacher modeled how a reader can use information to develop ideas about a text. The modeling move the teacher used is different from telling students the answer she wanted.

When modeling is folded briefly into ongoing discussions over time, it is a powerful way for students to encounter a range of expert reading behaviors. Moreover, modeling is particularly important in a QtA discussion because it reinforces for students the teacher's role as a collaborator in constructing meaning.

ANNOTATING

The discussion move we call annotating involves those instances during a discussion when a teacher provides information to fill in gaps. This is needed because sometimes authors do not provide enough information for students to be able to construct meaning from the text alone. There are gaps in information, holes in lines of reasoning, and assumptions about background knowledge that young readers do not have. To deal with such problems, teachers can use annotating.

To elaborate on the annotating move, we will look at some examples from a class of students who had been studying about the Whiskey Rebellion of the 1700s in the United States. The text provided very sparse information, so the teacher attempted to clarify an obscure text idea by saying, "The author doesn't really explain why the farmers made their corn into whiskey, but he gives us a hint when he says that whiskey could be transported long distances." The teacher tried to bring attention to a clue about the farmers' motives for making whiskey from their corn. The advantage for the farmers was that whiskey was easier to transport long distances than corn. The text information about this advantage was fairly obscure, and, therefore, the teacher used an annotating move to clarify the issue for students.

Another way to annotate text is to add information to the discussion. Consider another comment by the teacher:

> The author didn't tell us, but the Whiskey Rebellion was a real test of the new government. President Washington's decision to send troops to put down the rebellion was a message to the entire country.

This information is necessary if students are to construct an understanding of what made this event important. The teacher realized as the students were discussing this portion of text that they had no way of knowing why the author was treating this rebellion as something important, so she supplied the information.

RECAPPING

Recapping is a discussion move that is useful when students reach a place in their construction of ideas that indicates they have grasped the essential meaning and are ready to move on in the text and in the discussion. Recapping allows teachers to pull together and summarize major ideas that students have constructed up to a certain point. For example, the following comment signals students that they have accomplished something important and reinforces the understanding they have built:

> Those were great ideas. You figured out why the Eskimos moved so often in the winter even though the author did not explain it in the text.

Recapping also signals students that it is time to continue to a new or different point in the text. For example, a comment such as the following lets students know that the meaning they have constructed is part of a bigger picture that will come into focus only as they continue reading and discussing:

> Now that we've figured out why so many of the colonists were dissatisfied with the way Britain was treating them, let's see what they will do about it.

Recapping does not have to be the sole responsibility of the teacher. We have found that inviting students to recap is an effective way to encourage them to do the thinking and engage in the task of summarizing what has been constructed so far. In this way, students gain experience in capturing the most important ideas. Recapping encourages a mental organization of the ideas students have been grappling with and signals that the grappling has produced understanding.

DISCUSSION IN ACTION

In this section, we consider some lesson transcripts that further illustrate the discussion moves in action. The first transcript comes from a class in which students had been studying about the colonists in America. The text excerpt (Silver Burdett & Ginn, 1993, p. 156) that students read follows:

> The settlers chose a place on the bank of a river. They believed this place would be easy to defend. They built a fort, several houses, and a storehouse for food and supplies. They named the settlement Jamestown in honor of their king.
>
> The settlers of Jamestown could hardly have picked a worse spot to live. The land was low and swampy. This was a perfect place for disease-carrying mosquitoes to breed. The air, which was pleasant and warm in the spring, became hot and humid in the summer. Thick woods had to be cleared before planting could begin.

The teacher using QtA starts a discussion about this text with the following Initiating Query, which draws a rather sparse response:

Teacher: OK, what did the author tell us about this new colony called Jamestown?

Brooke: It was named after their king.

The teacher probes for more information, and the next student provides some additional details:

Teacher: OK. That's where it got its name. Did you pick up anything else?

Dorelle: It like had real bad lands. Like the swampy land got too hot and too much deep woods.

The teacher uses discussion moves by first revoicing Dorelle's response. Then he uses turning back to prompt the students to think about an apparent contradiction.

Teacher: So, Jamestown wasn't a very good place to live. But why would they choose a place like that?

Danisha: Because they thought it was easy to defend.

The teacher now marks Danisha's comment because he wants to emphasize that the defense notion is an important idea, one which students need to build an understanding of the logic behind the settlers' choice. But instead of explaining the logic himself, the teacher turns back the responsibility for constructing the idea to the students by asking, "Oh, so they thought it was easy to defend? Well, why would they choose a place they thought was easy to defend?" Responding to the focus of the teacher's Query, Leah introduces two important and related ideas:

Leah: I think that they did this because it was by the water and they needed a place that was easy to defend because the other colony just disappeared. So I think that they...um, wanted to be closest to water, so um they could run easily...like hop on the boat and leave.

The teacher sorts out Leah's ideas by revoicing her comments. In so doing, he assists students in connecting the two ideas:

Teacher: OK. So Leah says that they're a little concerned since the other colony before them disappeared and we don't know what happened to it. Something bad might have happened to those people. So something bad might happen again to these people. The settlers may need to escape fast so that's why they wanted to settle near the water.

Once the connection is made between access to water and the disappearance of the former colony, Nicole revoices the teacher's comment. Her comment seems to be an effort to explain why Jamestown was indeed a good choice for the settlers. Subsequently, this realization prompts a thoughtful and important question from Nicole:

Nicole: Well, that's smart 'cause they need to protect themselves 'cause they know something's happened to those other colonists. All that's wrong with this place is some mosquitoes, so why does the author say this couldn't be a worse place?

Nicole's question indicates a source of confusion. Although the author tells the reader about "disease-carrying mosquitoes," a young reader such as Nicole might have an understanding of mosquitoes that only accounts for them as sources of mild irritation and not as carriers of disease. The teacher recognizes that the author has not included any information about why mosquitoes would be considered more dangerous to people several hundred years ago than they are today, and he also realizes that Nicole's question reveals confusion about why mosquitoes are an issue of danger. Because the author provides no information to help students sort out the confusion, the teacher responds by annotating:

Teacher: Oh, good question. The author doesn't really tell us why mosquitoes are a problem, but mosquitoes are dangerous carriers of disease. Back then, there were no antibiotics for infections as we have today. So, if someone became ill from mosquito bites, there would be no way to treat or cure them. The settlers would be more afraid of mosquitoes in their time than we would be today.

The use of annotating allowed the teacher to provide important information and facilitate building an understanding of ideas that otherwise might not have been possible for students to do on their own.

Now we will look at another transcript for an idea of how the discussion moves played out in a different lesson. The short passage that follows was being read during a social studies class (Wallower & Wholey, p. 41):

> Washington gave the Governor's letter to the French leader. No one knew this, but Washington made a drawing of the fort. Washington saw that the French planned to make war on the English. At last, the French leader gave Washington a message for the Governor. He said that the French would not leave Pennsylvania.

The teacher begins with an Initiating Query to direct students' attention to the important ideas in the passage, and a student responds with one of the important issues:

Teacher: So, what's the author's message here?

Quianna: That, um, the French aren't gonna leave Pennsylvania. And they just plan to keep it.

The teacher revoices Quianna's comment and then asks the other students to consider the source of Quianna's idea:

Teacher: The French plan to keep it for themselves. What's the author say to make Quianna think that?

Dorelle: They were planning to stay, and I think that they're bound to have a war.

The teacher highlights Dorelle's comment by marking it, and at the same time, she uses turning back to encourage other students to think about why and how Dorelle came to that idea:

Teacher: Dorelle said that they were bound to have a war. Hmm. What do you think gave Dorelle that idea?

Leah: Because the governor knew that, um, the French were staying because, um, I think he knew that the French wouldn't just let the English have it without having a war.

The teacher uses revoicing to clarify and elaborate on Leah's comment, which then prompts more thinking. The contributions of the next two students extend and support the comments of Dorelle and Leah:

Teacher: So, you think it was just stupid that all the British governor would have to say is "Please leave," and the French would say, "OK, I'll just pack my bags and go." I think Leah is right—that wouldn't happen because there is too much at stake and there would probably be war.

Johnny: They have soldiers, so why would they leave when they have the soldiers there to fight?

Terrell: I think that, if the English try to make another move on the French, there's definitely gonna be a war. And the last person there is gonna keep the land.

Having some evidence that students have grasped the situation of pending war and the tensions surrounding it, the teacher moves on to point out a specific portion of the text that implicitly deals with the tensions of war. However, this is followed by a student's response that omits any reference to these tensions:

Teacher: OK. Very good. Now I want to draw your attention to a place in the text that says "No one knew this, but Washington made a drawing of the fort." Hmm. Why do you think the author tells us this? What is this drawing of the fort all about?

Curtis:	'Cause when he gives the message to the governor...the reason is he wants him to know what the fort looks like.

The teacher marks Curtis's rather flat response in a way that suggests there is a deeper issue behind Washington's drawing of the forts. She then turns back the responsibility to the students for figuring out what that deeper issue might be. The next two students move toward defining the issue in their responses, which the teacher then revoices:

Teacher:	Oh, so Washington was drawing the fort for a reason then, to show the governor? But why would he want to show the governor what the fort looked like anyway?
Joey:	Maybe because the governor would need to know what the fort looked like, like how big it was.
Curtis:	Yeah...so when he attacked, he'd know where to attack the fort and how many soldiers and how much stuff he'd need to do it with.
Teacher:	That makes sense. I think Joey and Curtis are saying that if the English wanted to go to war, they'd have to plan where they'd have to attack the fort and how many soldiers they would need to be successful. Washington knew this and that's why he drew the map.

Notice the comment that this discussion produces from Leah:

Leah:	Did you notice that every story we read like this, it's like the author makes something sound stupid at first, but then it's really not? Sometimes we figure things out and see that things he says aren't stupid, but make sense.

Leah's question and comment say it all. As a result of having to "figure things out," the students seem to discover that with enough attention and work, they are able to construct meaning and understanding themselves from otherwise confusing texts.

RECAPPING DISCUSSION

Discussion is at the heart of QtA, but a QtA discussion is more than just the teacher posing Queries and students responding to them. Because discussion is dynamic and somewhat unpredictable, teachers need tools to manage discussion—to orchestrate student ideas and make improvisational decisions during a discussion. We call these tools discussion moves, and we have identified six.

Marking involves drawing attention to an idea to emphasize its importance and to use it as a basis for further discussion. Turning back can involve turning back to students the responsibility for thinking through and figuring out ideas or turning back to text as a source for clarifying thinking and keeping discussion on track. In revoicing, a teacher interprets what students are struggling to express and rephrases ideas so they can become part of the discussion. Marking, turning back, and revoicing represent different ways to make productive use of what students offer in a discussion .

The next three moves, modeling, annotating, and recapping, involve greater teacher input in the discussion. The teacher steps into the discussion in a more direct way. Modeling makes public the processes in which readers engage in the course of reading. We believe that modeling is most effective when it is kept short and is folded into discussions to emphasize an authentic response to text. Annotating involves providing information to fill in gaps or point out sources of confusion in a text. When recapping, a teacher reviews or highlights major ideas and understandings learned up to a specific point in the text. Over time, students can assume more responsibility for recapping.

The discussion moves allow teachers to distribute the work of constructing meaning from a text by making use of student ideas even when those ideas are not completely formed. The moves also allow teachers to assume more of a role in supporting meaning making when such support is needed.

CHAPTER 5

IMPLEMENTATION

The major focus in getting started with Questioning the Author (QtA) in the classroom is preparing students for a new way of thinking about reading and of responding to their texts and to one another in discussion. Before turning to these issues, however, the physical setup of the classroom deserves some attention. Because QtA uses discussion as a context for encouraging students to collaboratively construct meaning, it is helpful if the desks in the classroom are arranged to facilitate discussion. We have found that arranging student seats in a large *U* shape seems to work well. This arrangement helps students see and interact with one another more easily. It also facilitates teacher movement among students during a discussion.

In the rest of this chapter, we offer some of the wording that we and other teachers have used to introduce QtA to students. What we provide is intended only to help capture the kinds of information that should be presented to students.

GETTING STARTED

To get students started with QtA, it is important to tell them that they will be taking part in a different type of reading from what they might have known before. This might be accomplished by saying something like: "This year when we read, we're going to do things differently from the way you are probably used to doing them. So today, I'd like to talk to you about what I mean by this different way of reading." The intent is to get students ready for something new.

Our experience has shown us that it is very useful to introduce the notion of author fallibility in a direct way to students. Setting forth the idea that texts are merely someone's ideas written down might be approached as follows:

> One important idea to remember about reading is that what we read is just someone's ideas written down—someone called an author. Sometimes what authors have in their minds to say just doesn't come through clearly when they write about it. Authors are real people, so, just like real people, they aren't perfect. Sometimes authors do a fine job of explaining something, but other times, they don't do a very good job at all. As readers, we have a job to do. We have to figure out what the author is trying to explain.

It is important to communicate that authors may not express their ideas clearly so readers have to work to understand what authors are trying to say. Thus, a major goal in introducing QtA is to directly address the tendency of students to blame themselves for not being able to understand information in a text in which the author did not express his or her ideas clearly enough to be understood. We have found it useful to tell students explicitly and repeatedly that it is their job to judge an author's success in making ideas clear to them. When students understand this concept, they appear to be more inclined to grapple with a text's ideas to make sense of what is there. Because the fear of being wrong has been reduced, understanding a text becomes more an opportunity for an exciting collaborative challenge and less a threatening, sometimes defeating, individual chore. The result typically is more excitement and cooperation.

Another point to make explicit to students is why authors are sometimes difficult to understand. Students need to know some of the reasons texts can seem confusing and difficult so that they can begin to recognize problems of incoherence and density of presentation themselves. An explanation might resemble this:

> Sometimes, when adults try to write something to explain some new information to kids, they aren't always able to explain it really well for someone who doesn't already know the stuff.

The important message is that students hear the teacher say specifically why texts might be confusing and difficult. Such an explanation can reduce student defensiveness about not understanding.

THINKING ALOUD ABOUT TEXT

After letting students know that they will be engaging in a different kind of reading and discussion, and introducing the notion of author fallibility, the next step that we have used to prepare students for the QtA orientation is a model text and exercise that we developed known as "A Russian Traveler." The exercise is a think-aloud of a brief text in which the teacher demonstrates the kind of consideration and grappling that characterizes reading in QtA. The text for the exercise is about Russia's launching of the first satellite into space, as follows:

A Russian Traveler

The day is Friday, October 4. The year is 1957. People in many parts of the earth turned on radios and heard strange news. "Russia has used rockets to put a new moon in the sky," said one station. "The tiny moon is a metal ball. It has a radio in it. The radio goes 'beep! beep! beep!' as the moon travels along. The new moon is named Sputnik. *Sputnik* is a word that means traveler in Russian."

A month later, radios sent out more exciting news. "Russian rockets have carried a small spaceship into space," they said. "The ship is just big enough to carry a little dog. The ship sends out signals about the dog. The signals will help us learn if animals can live in space."

Everywhere people became interested in rockets and spaceships.

When we have used "A Russian Traveler" to demonstrate thinking about reading, we have introduced it by saying something like this:

So, when we read something, if we're really going to put the ideas together so we understand what we read, we have to work and figure it out as we go along. You can think of it as a little like talking to yourself about what you're reading, and deciding whether the ideas are clear. Let me show you what I mean about thinking through what an author is trying to say as you read. To do this, I'll use a short piece of text from a social studies textbook, because it has some things in it that seem pretty confusing at first.

We have developed segmented portions of the Russian Traveler text and a corresponding script that can be used as a model. The goal is to convey to students two voices: one is the author's words from the text, italicized in the passage that follows; the other is the reader's voice, mulling over the author's words in an effort to make sense of those ideas. The reader's voice is represented in the passage in quotation marks. When the Russian Traveler script is used, students should be given a copy of the text so they can follow along as the reader thinks aloud. Here is how it might sound:

> *A Russian Traveler* "Hmmm...someone from Russia must be going somewhere."
> *The day is Friday, October 4. The year is 1957.* "OK, so I know something about a date and time."

Continue in this same way, reading and then stopping to think aloud:

> *People in many parts of the earth turned on radios and heard strange news.* "I think the author is trying to tell us that something important happened."
> *"Russia has used rockets to put a new moon in the sky," said one station.* "Hmm. I don't know what the author means. How can you put up another moon?"
> *The tiny moon is a metal ball. It has a radio in it. The radio goes 'beep! beep! beep!' as the moon travels along.* "I don't know what the author is trying to tell us about...how can a metal ball with a radio in it be a moon?"

At this point in the text, students should be given an opportunity to say if the concept seems confusing to them as well. Then, the demonstration can continue as follows:

> *The new moon is named Sputnik. Sputnik is a word that means traveler in Russian.* "Now I think I know what the author is getting at. You might not know this, but I remember that there was a Russian satellite or spaceship called Sputnik. Maybe that's what the author means when he says "a new moon"—a satellite

---

in space! I think the author could have explained this better because kids are going to be reading this and they may never have heard of Sputnik before."

A month later, radios sent out more exciting news. "Russian rockets have carried a small spaceship into space," they said. "Here, the author is being clearer...talking about a spaceship rather than a moon with a radio."

The ship is just big enough to carry a little dog. "So it must not be a very big spaceship."

The ship sends out signals about the dog. "Oh! There is a dog on the spaceship! I thought they just meant that's what size it was—big enough for a dog!"

At this point, students might be asked if they understood there was a dog on board or thought the reference to the dog was just an indicator of size. Then, reading the text can be resumed:

The signals will help us learn if animals can live in space. "Hmmm, what does the author mean, signals could help us learn if animals could live in space? He doesn't say what kind of signals—what kind of signal could do that, do you think?"

Here might be another good place to elicit student reactions. Then, reading the text can resume:

Everywhere people became interested in rockets and spaceships. "This last sentence seems like a big jump from talking about the dog. I guess maybe the author is trying to connect the ending sentence with the beginning sentence about people all over the world turning on their radios."

After students have interacted with "A Russian Traveler," a discussion might be initiated to encourage them to notice various features of the reading and thinking experience. The discussion might start with something like this:

> So, did that give you any ideas about how things are written sometimes? Sometimes an author makes things pretty clear, and then other things aren't said in a very clear way at all—like calling the satellite a "new moon." Did anyone have any other questions or see anything confusing as we read along?

As students respond, they should be encouraged to give specific examples from the text. Their responses can be followed by asking them what they think the author was trying to say or what they think the author meant.

The purpose of presenting "A Russian Traveler" is to begin to help students become aware of the kinds of thinking and work it takes to construct meaning from text. The demonstration is intended to help students understand what is different about QtA reading and to emphasize that authors do not always communicate information clearly, which can make text difficult to understand.

LINKING THE DEMONSTRATION AND DAILY DISCUSSIONS

The experience with "A Russian Traveler" can be linked to what will be done regularly in QtA discussions, as follows:

> So what we just did with the Russian traveler text gives you some idea about how we're going to do our reading in class this year. The important thing is to work out ideas as we read along in a text. When we read together, I will stop the reading every now and then to start us thinking about what we're reading and to make sure we're figuring it out so we understand what the author is trying to say. What we'll be doing as we go along is saying things like: "OK what did the au-

thor mean by that?" or "Why did the author say that?" or "Why is that important for us to know?"

The initial introduction of QtA might be concluded by saying something like: "Remember that authors are just people putting their ideas on paper. As readers, our job is to figure out those ideas. When we do this, we'll be doing something called 'Questioning the Author'."

RECAPPING IMPLEMENTATION

To conclude, explicitly signaling to students that they are going to be thinking about text in a new way is an important first step in implementing QtA. Using a think-aloud demonstration is one way to do this directly. Another way to let students know that their participation and collaboration in the process of meaning making is important is arranging the desks in the classroom in a way that facilitates discussion. This rearrangement is a very strong cue to students that their involvement in thinking and talking about text is the goal of QtA.

CHAPTER 6

WHERE HAS QUESTIONING THE AUTHOR BEEN AND WHERE IS IT GOING?

This chapter will first look at the history of Questioning the Author (QtA) in the classrooms in which it has been implemented and then look forward to where the project is headed.

WHERE HAS QUESTIONING THE AUTHOR BEEN?

QtA has been implemented over 3 years in the classrooms of five teachers and with about 120 fourth- and fifth-grade students in two different school districts. Some of the teachers are now in their fourth year of using QtA. The result has been dramatic changes in classroom discourse. The findings come from comparing both reading and social studies lessons that were taught by the collaborating teachers before and after they implemented QtA. (For a full discussion of these results see Beck et al., 1996; McKeown, Beck, & Sandora, 1996.) The changes include the following:

- Teachers ask questions that focus on considering and extending meaning rather than retrieving information.
- Teachers respond to students in ways that extend the conversation rather than simply evaluating or repeating the responses.
- Students do about twice as much talking during QtA discussions than they did in traditional lessons.
- Students frequently initiate their own questions and comments in contrast to rarely doing so in traditional lessons.
- Students respond by talking about the meaning of what they read and by integrating ideas rather than by retrieving text information.
- Student-to-student interactions during discussions are common.

QtA also has been effective with older students and in contrast to another discussion technique, Junior Great Books. In a study that compared QtA with Junior Great Books, in which discussion was done only after reading whole text selections, sixth- and seventh-grade students in the QtA condition both recalled more from each selection and were better able to provide high-quality responses to interpretation questions (Sandora, 1994).

In our work with QtA, we have talked extensively with the teachers about their experiences and also have interviewed the students to find out their views. We learned that as the teachers began implementation, they were concerned about the impact of using QtA on their classroom management. As the year progressed, they found that not only was it possible to "share control of the discussion with students and not lose acceptable classroom decorum in the process," as one teacher said, but also the involvement of students in ideas became an exciting and extremely satisfying aspect of classroom lessons. Teachers eventually found that classroom management was less of a concern during QtA lessons because the students became so involved in the issues of the discussion.

The teachers also talked about how their expectations of their students had changed as they observed them dealing with ideas and expressing themselves in QtA discussions. One teacher commented that she now expected her students to "think, learn, and explain rather than memorize, dictate, and forget."

Students' views about reading and learning also have been affected. We saw evidence of these changes in responses students gave when we interviewed them at the end of the school year and asked them to describe their reading and social studies classes. One student talked about the need for the kind of thinking and questioning that the class did:

> Sometimes when the author is not being real clear, it's kind of hard because then in the way back of the story is a sentence that you need to figure out and put the clues together, but you don't have all the clues.

She then described what happened as a result of working to figure out the ideas:

> So we understand what the author's really telling us instead of just reading the story and saying we're done.

Another student described her view of reading in QtA as follows:

It's more creative than just asking regular questions or just plain reading you know, like if you don't think about what you're reading and you just read, that's not reading. You're just looking at scribbles on a piece of paper. You know.

WHERE IS QUESTIONING THE AUTHOR GOING?

In QtA, the discourse between students and teacher and among students is the substance from which meaning is built. Yet group talk will not necessarily lead to meaning building. Discourse that leads to meaning building needs direction, focus, and movement toward a goal. To effectively foster such discourse, a teacher must not only attend to the content of what is being read and the ideas important for building meaning from that content, but also monitor where students are in the construction process and then pull from that combination of factors ways to direct the dialogue to promote understanding. As Cazden (1988) says, "It is easy to imagine talk in which ideas are explored rather than answers to teachers' test questions provided and evaluated.... Easy to imagine, but not easy to do" (p. 54).

We have come to understand very clearly how much effort and attention it takes to change one's teaching practices to a more constructivist orientation. Our new direction is to take advantage of all we have learned in working with our collaborating teachers and transform that knowledge into forms that other teachers can use. Our approach to transforming the knowledge we have gained involves creating resources to support teachers as they work with QtA in their classrooms. Although we have developed a workshop to introduce teachers to QtA, we are convinced that the work we need to do is determine how to support teachers as they attempt to change their teaching practices day by day.

The development of effective support materials calls for understanding and anticipating pitfalls that teachers encounter as they move toward constructivist practice and the design of resources to help teachers address those situations. The resources we are developing, in the form of printed materials and videotape segments, are based on actual classroom interactions and issues that concerned teachers during QtA implementations. These "accessibles," as we call them, present specific classroom discussion situations, accompanied by explanatory annotations that set up a problem or issue, draw attention to how the issue developed, and provide examples of ways the issue might be dealt with. The interaction of examples and annotations operates at the intersection of understanding and actions. Thus, the accessibles avoid the problems of scripted "cookbook" type lesson plans that put words into teachers' mouths and connect only with actions, and of general principles that have only vague connections to useful teaching practices.

We will explore the effectiveness of the accessibles by closely following teachers as they implement QtA using the resources as support materials. This exploration will include frequent observations, videotaping, and interviews with teachers about their use of the resources. We will then use the information we gather to evaluate and refine the materials for broader use. Our principal concern is to create resources that provide effective ongoing support, because it is in the day-to-day student-teacher classroom interactions that the real work of changing practice occurs.

REFERENCES

Anderson, R.C. (1977). The notion of schemata and the educational enterprise. In R.C. Anderson, R.J. Spiro, & W.E. Montague (Eds.), *Schooling and the acquisition of knowledge* (pp. 415–431). Hillsdale, NJ: Erlbaum.

Anderson, R.C., Chinn, C., Commeyras, M., Stallman, A., Waggoner, M., & Wilkinson, I. (1992, December). The reflective thinking project. In K. Jongsma (Chair), *Understanding and enhancing literature discussion in elementary classrooms.* Symposium conducted at the 42nd Annual Meeting of the National Reading Conference, San Antonio, TX.

Anderson, R.C., Reynolds, R.E., Schallert, D.L., & Goetz, E.T. (1977). Frameworks for comprehending discourse. *American Educational Research Journal, 14,* 367–382.

Beck, I.L. (1989). Improving practice through understanding reading. In L. Resnick & L. Klopfer (Eds.), *Toward the thinking curriculum: Current cognitive research* (pp. 40–58). Alexandria, VA: Association for Supervision and Curriculum Development.

Beck, I.L., & Carpenter, P.A. (1986). Cognitive approaches to understanding reading: Implications for instructional practice. *American Psychologist, 41*(10), 1098–1105.

Beck, I.L., & McKeown, M.G. (1981). Developing questions that promote comprehension. *Language Arts, 58*, 913–918.

Beck, I.L., McKeown, M.G., & Gromoll, E.W. (1989). Learning from social studies texts. *Cognition and Instruction, 6*, 99–158.

Beck, I.L., McKeown, M.G., & Omanson, R. (1987). The effects and uses of diverse vocabulary instructional techniques. In M.G. McKeown & M.E. Curtis (Eds.), *The nature of vocabulary acquisition* (pp. 147–163). Hillsdale, NJ: Erlbaum.

Beck, I.L., McKeown, M.G., & Sinatra, G.M. (1989). *The representations that fifth graders develop about the American revolutionary period from reading social studies textbooks.* Unpublished manuscript.

Beck, I.L., McKeown, M.G., Sinatra, G.M., & Loxterman, J.A. (1991). Revising social studies text from a text-processing perspective: Evidence of improved comprehensibility. *Reading Research Quarterly, 26*, 251–276.

Beck, I.L., McKeown, M.G., Worthy, J., Sandora, C.A., & Kucan, L. (1996). Questioning the Author: A year-long classroom implementation to engage students with text. *The Elementary School Journal, 96*(4), 385–414.

Beck, I.L., Omanson, R., & McKeown, M.G. (1982). An instructional redesign of reading lessons: Effects on comprehension. *Reading Research Quarterly, 17*, 462–481.

Black, J.B., & Bern, H. (1981). Causal coherence and memory for events in narratives. *Journal of Verbal Learning and Verbal Behavior, 20*, 267–275.

Bransford, J.D., & Johnson, M.K. (1973). Contextual prerequisites for understanding: Some investigations of comprehension and recall. *Journal of Verbal Learning and Verbal Behavior, 11*, 717–726.

Bruer, J.T. (1993). *Schools for thought: A science of learning in the classroom.* Cambridge, MA: MIT Press.

Carver, R.P. (1987). Should reading comprehension skills be taught? In J.E. Readance & R.S. Baldwin (Eds.), *Research in literacy: Merging perspectives* (Thirty-sixth Yearbook of the National Reading Conference, pp. 115–126). Rochester, NY: National Reading Conference.

Cazden, C.B. (1988). *Classroom discourse: The language of teaching and learning.* Portsmouth, NH: Heinemann.

Chi, M.T.H., Bassok, M., Lewis, M., Reimann, P., & Glaser, R. (1989). Self-explanations: How students study and use examples in learning to solve problems. *Cognitive Science, 13*, 45–182.

Chi, M.T.H., de Leeuw, N., Chiu, M., & LaVancher, C. (1994). Eliciting self-explanations improves understanding. *Cognitive Science, 18,* 439–477.

Clark, H.H. (1977). Inferences in comprehension. In D. LaBerge & S.J. Samuels (Eds.), *Basic processing in reading: Perception and comprehension* (pp. 243–263). Hillsdale, NJ: Erlbaum.

Clark, H.H., & Haviland, S.E. (1977). Comprehension and the given-new contract. In R.O. Freedle (Ed.), *Discourse production and comprehension* (pp. 1–40). Norwood, NJ: Ablex.

Cohen, D.K., McLaughlin, M.W., & Talbert, J. (Eds.). (1993). *Teaching for understanding.* San Francisco, CA: Jossey-Bass.

Denis, R., & Moldof, G. (1983). *A handbook on interpretive reading and discussion.* Chicago, IL: Great Books Foundation.

Dillon, J.T. (1988). *Questioning and teaching: A manual of practice.* New York: Teachers College Press.

Dole, J.A., Duffy, G.G., Roehler, L.R., & Pearson, P.D. (1991). Moving from the old to the new: Research on reading comprehension instruction. *Review of Educational Research, 61,* 239–264.

Duffy, G.G., Roehler, L.R., & Herrmann, B.A. (1988). Modeling mental processes helps poor readers become strategic readers. *The Reading Teacher, 41,* 762–767.

Duffy, G.G., et al. (1987). Effects of explaining the reasoning associated with using reading strategies. *Reading Research Quarterly, 22,* 347–368.

Gardner, H. (1985). *The mind's new science.* New York: Basic Books.

Gaskins, I.W., Anderson, R.C., Pressley, M., Cunicelli, M., & Satlow, E. (1993). Six teachers' dialogue during cognitive process instruction. *The Elementary School Journal, 93,* 277–304.

Goldenberg, C. (1992). Instructional conversations: Promoting comprehension through discussion. *The Reading Teacher, 46,* 316–326.

Haviland, S.E., & Clark, H.H. (1974). What's new? Acquiring new information as a process in comprehension. *Journal of Verbal Learning and Verbal Behavior, 13,* 512–521.

Just, M.A., & Carpenter, P.A. (1987). *The psychology of reading and language comprehension.* Rockleigh, NJ: Allyn & Bacon.

Kieras, D.E. (1985). Thematic processes in the comprehension of technical prose. In B.K. Britton & J.B. Black, (Eds.), *Understanding expository text: A theoretical and practical handbook for analyzing explanatory text* (pp. 89–107). Hillsdale, NJ: Erlbaum.

Kintsch, W., & Keenan, J.M. (1973). Reading rate as a function of the number of propositions in the base structure of sentences. *Cognitive Psychology, 5,* 257–274.

Laidlaw. (1985). *Living in world regions.* River Forest, IL: Author.

Luke, C., DeCastell, S., & Luke, A. (1983). Beyond criticism: The authority of the school text. *Curriculum Inquiry, 13,* 111–127.

McGilly, K. (Ed.). (1994). *Classroom lessons: Integrating cognitive theory and classroom practice.* Cambridge, MA: MIT Press.

McKeown, M.G., Beck, I.L, & Sandora, C.A. (1996). Questioning the Author: An approach to developing meaningful classroom discourse. In M.G. Graves, P. van den Broek, & B.M. Taylor (Eds.), *The first R: Every child's right to read* (pp. 97–119). New York: Teachers College Press; Newark, DE: International Reading Association.

McMahon, S.I., Raphael, T.E., Goatley, V.S., Boyd, F.B., & Pardo, L.S. (1992, December). The reflective thinking project. In K. Jongsma (Chair), *Understanding and enhancing literature discussion in elementary classrooms.* Symposium conducted at the 42nd Annual Meeting of the National Reading Conference, San Antonio, TX.

Mehan, H. (1979). *Learning lessons: Social organization in the classroom.* Cambridge, MA: Harvard University Press.

Newman, D., Griffin, P., & Cole, M. (1989). *The construction zone: Working for cognitive change in school.* Cambridge, UK: Cambridge University Press.

O'Flahavan, J.F., & Stein, C. (1992, December). The conversational discussion groups project. In K. Jongsma (Chair), *Understanding and enhancing literature discussion in elementary classrooms.* Symposium conducted at the 42nd Annual Meeting of the National Reading Conference, San Antonio, TX.

Olson, D.R. (1980). On the language and authority of textbooks. *Journal of Communication, 30,* 186–196.

Omanson, R.C., Beck, I.L., McKeown, M.G., & Perfetti, C.A. (1984). Comprehension of texts with unfamiliar versus recently taught words: Assessment of alternative models. *Journal of Educational Psychology, 76,* 1253–1268.

Palincsar, A.S., & Brown, A.L. (1984). Reciprocal teaching of comprehension-fostering and comprehension-monitoring activities. *Cognition and Instruction, 1,* 117–175.

Palincsar, A.S., & Brown, A.L. (1989). Instruction for self-regulated reading. In L. Resnick & L. Klopfer (Eds.), *Toward the thinking curriculum: Current cognitive research* (pp. 19–39). Alexandria, VA: Association for Supervision and Curriculum Development.

Paris, S.G., Cross, D.R., & Lipson, M.Y. (1984). Informed strategies for learning: A program to improve children's awareness and comprehension. *Journal of Educational Psychology, 76,* 1239–1252.

Pearson, P.D., & Fielding, L. (1991). Comprehension instruction. In R. Barr, M. Kamil, P. Mosenthal, & P.D. Pearson (Eds.), *Handbook of reading research: Volume II* (pp. 815–860). White Plains, NY: Longman.

Pearson, P.D., Hansen, J., & Gordon, C. (1979). The effect of background knowledge on young children's comprehension of explicit and implicit information. *Journal of Reading Behavior, 11*, 201–209.

Perfetti, C.A. (1985). *Reading ability.* New York: Oxford University Press.

Prawat, R.S. (1992). Teachers' beliefs about teaching and learning: A constructivist perspective. *American Journal of Education, 100*, 354–395.

Pressley, M., et al. (1992). Beyond direct explanation: Transactional instruction of reading comprehension strategies. *The Elementary School Journal, 92*, 511–553.

Resnick, L.B., & Klopfer, L.E. (1989). *Toward the thinking curriculum: Current cognitive research.* Alexandria, VA: Association for Supervision and Curriculum Development.

Rumelhart, D.E. (1980). Schemata: The building blocks of cognition. In R.J. Spiro, B.C. Bruce, & W.F. Brewer (Eds.), *Theoretical issues in reading comprehension* (pp. 35–58). Hillsdale, NJ: Erlbaum.

Sandora, C.A. (1994). *A comparison of two discussion techniques: Great Books (post-reading) and Questioning the Author (on-line) on students' comprehension and interpretation of narrative texts.* Unpublished doctoral dissertation, University of Pittsburgh, Pittsburgh, PA.

Schank, R.C., & Abelson, R.P. (1977). *Scripts, plans, goals, and understanding.* Hillsdale, NJ: Erlbaum.

Silver Burdett & Ginn. (1985). *The United States and its neighbors.* Morristown, NJ: Author.

Silver Burdett & Ginn. (1989). *The world of reading.* Morristown, NJ: Author.

Silver Burdett & Ginn. (1990). *Pennsylvania yesterday and today.* Morristown, NJ: Author.

Silver Burdett & Ginn. (1993). *Our country.* Morristown, NJ: Author.

Trabasso, T., Secco, T., & van den Broek, P. (1984). Causal cohesion and story coherence. In H. Mandl, N.L. Stein, & T. Trabasso (Eds.), *Learning and comprehension of text* (pp. 83–111). Hillsdale, NJ: Erlbaum.

van Dijk, T.A., & Kintsch, W. (1983). *Strategies of discourse comprehension.* New York: Academic Press.

Wallower, L., & Wholey, E.J. (1984). *All about Pennsylvania.* Harrisburg, PA: Penns Valley.

AUTHOR INDEX

A
Abelson, R.P., 9, 118
Almasi, J., 118
Anderson, R.C., 9, 14, 15, 114, 116
Armbruster, B.B., v

B
Bassok, M., 115
Beck, I.L., iv, 8, 9, 14, 15, 48, 110, 114, 115, 117
Bergman, J.L., 118
Bern, H., 14, 115
Black, J.B., 14, 115
Boyd, F.B., 117
Bransford, J.D., 14, 115
Brown, A.L., 9, 16, 117
Brown, R., 118
Bruer, J.T., 8, 115

C
Carpenter, P.A., 8, 9, 13, 115, 116
Carver, R.P., 16, 115
Cazden, C.B., 112, 115
Chi, M.T.H., 16, 115, 116
Chinn, C., 114
Chiu, M., 116
Clark, H.H., 9, 14, 116
Cleary, B., 82
Cohen, D.K., 8, 116
Cole, M., 9, 117
Commeyras, M., 114
Cross, D.R., 16, 117
Cunicelli, M., 116

D
de Leeuw, N., 116

DeCastell, S., 18, 117
Denis, R., 16, 116
Dillon, J.T., 23, 116
Dole, J.A., 16, 116
Duffy, G.G., 16, 87, 116

E–F
El-Dinary, P.B., 118
Fielding, L., 16, 117
Forbes, K., 12

G
Gardner, H., 8, 116
Gaskins, I.W., 16, 116, 118
Glaser, R., 115
Goatley, V.S., 117
Goetz, E.T., 114
Goldenberg, C., 15, 116
Gordon, C., 14, 118
Griffin, P., 9, 117
Gromoll, E.W., 14, 48, 115

H
Hansen, J., 14, 118
Haviland, S.E., 9, 14, 116
Herrmann, B.A., 87, 116

J
Johnson, M.K., 14, 115
Just, M.A., 13, 116

K
Keenan, J.M., 14, 116
Kieras, D.E., 9, 116
Kintsch, W., 9, 14, 116, 118
Klopfer, L.E., 9, 118
Kucan, L., 115

SUBJECT INDEX

Note: An "*f*" following a page number indicates that the reference may be found in a figure; a "*t*" indicates that it may be found in a table.